CW01210723

NORSE MAGIC, RUNES & MYTHOLOGY

LEARN THE ARCANE SECRETS OF NORSE PAGANISM, RUNIC MAGIC, AND DEEP DIVE INTO VIKING FOLKLORE OF NORSE GODS, GODDESSES, AND MYTHOLOGY!

EMMA KARLSSON

FREE GIFT JUST FOR YOU!

FREE 2024 NORSE GOD & GODDESSES CALENDAR
Use this link https://bit.ly/4a44HzY

OR scan the QR code below:

CONTENTS

AN INTRODUCTION TO NORSE MAGIC

"I know that I hung
on the wind-swept tree
all nine nights
with a spear was I wounded
and given to Odin,
myself to me,
on that tree which no one knows
from which roots it grows."

Odin, The Prose Edda.

Language, Mystery, Magic, and More

The world around is abound with magic and mystery, with everything possessing a deeper reality than meets the eye. A lake where families gather for picnics may as well be used by someone initiated to the ways of witchcraft to scry the future on the surface of the water. The same clouds that are the portents of joy for a farmer can very well be omens of doom for a shaman.

There are deeper realities than ours. Trees speak to each other in the silence of the forest in secret tongues. The dead hold long talks in the solitude of their graves. Old gods, seated on their thrones, hold discourse in holy languages. At every level, even at the subatomic level of quarks and photons, communication takes place in some language or the other.

Language

It remains an alluring concept in multiple disciplines, whether it's the science of linguistics or the study of ancient civilizations by archeologists. Language, despite being the very tool that uncovers truths and bridges distances, retains its certain shares of mysteries.

Such as where did it come from? Did it evolve over the course of thousands of years from the barbaric caws and yaps of cave-people to this sophisticated tool of nuanced diction and grammar, or did it descend upon us as a revelation from some cosmic source?

Is the nature of language one-dimensional, where words are only used to convey your thoughts, or is there something much more profound at work where words, if spoken with the right intent and inflection, can alter the fabric of nature in a phenomenon known as magic?

If so, does each of us preternaturally possess a propensity toward this paranormal power?

Here, I would like you to take a leap of faith with me and believe that, yes, there *is* something much more profound at work, that we *do* possess an innate albeit mostly dormant talent to harness that power, and that, *yes,* language, besides its natural evolution, did descend upon us from a cosmic source.

Suspend your disbelief, kindle the seeker within, and come with me on a journey that shall take us through time and space into a world of magic, paganism, runes, myth, and mystery. It is a world of Norse magic, paganism, runes, rituals, and powerful gods and goddesses.

A Tale of Sacrifice

I would very much like to begin this book by telling you a story.

A story about a blue-eyed wanderer, a bearded traveler wielding a cane that bears resemblance on second glance to a spear. This lone figure, you can tell, is weathered but not beaten. He has seen much, and much has he braved. Two ravens circle him as he walks, and two wolves trail his steps, ever his eager and loyal companions.

Do not make the mistake of assuming that it is some common mortal. He goes by many monikers and titles. The god of war, for one. The lord of all kingship. He has gone to the most extreme lengths to secure the most arcane magic and archaic knowledge.

What made him a god, perhaps, apart from his omnipotent abilities and his omniscience, was his unquenchable thirst for knowledge. A mortal would have called it quits after reaching a certain point, comfortable that he had learned it all, seen it all, done it all, but not Odin.

Philosophers like Plato and Socrates have often remarked that one of the most humbling aspects of learning includes the realization that you, even after knowing all that you know, don't know anything at all. That the vast sea of unknown far outweighs the bottled known you hold in your hands.

Perhaps it was that same philosophical realization embedded deep within Odin, or perhaps it was that he had to deal with primal forces of nature, almost as powerful as the god himself, sometimes intangible and elusive, to attain sacred knowledge.

For instance, he once stole the Mead of Poetry by taking the shape of an eagle, and once he visited a place of no return, the realm of Hel, to learn about the end of the world from a dead seer.

Apart from the big picture stuff, his two ravens were always flying across the Nine Realms to find out everything they could about what was happening in those worlds, and they would report to him daily.

When Odin's paths came to a drastic crossroads in his quest for knowledge, Odin did not hesitate in sacrificing his own eye to acquire the knowledge from Mimir's well.

He kept a watchful eye on the Norns, the beings who controlled fate and wove the past, present, and future of every being, and learned that they knew more about fate and matters of destiny than anyone else in the world. He observed how they wove fate from the Well of Urd at the roots of Yggdrasil. Odin had great regard for fate and knew that it was such a central force of nature that nothing could avert it.

At this point in our story, Odin stands at the precipice of the Well, contemplating the nature of the sacrifice he has to offer to attain some wisdom from this mysterious and secretive well.

After much meditation, it comes to him. He decides to offer himself as a sacrifice by hanging from the branches of Yggdrasil and piercing himself with his spear.

He hangs like this, in unbearable agony, for nine days and nights. To him, this is a very reasonable sacrifice in exchange for the wisdom of the well and the knowledge of the Norns.

The creatures of the Yggdrasil come to him and try to help him. The eagle, who sits at the top, and the squirrel Ratatoskr who climbs up and down the tree both offer him food and water, but Odin, stalwart in his goal, perseveres without aid.

It is at this point that the Well of Urd takes notice and acknowledges the sacrifice, slowly starting to reveal its knowledge. At first, nine songs are taught to him that contain nine words of power.

Odin can stop here. He knows this. But if he stops, the Well would stop too. So, Odin perseveres harder, and by the end of the ninth day, when he's on the verge of death, the Well of Urd accepts his sacrifice and reveals to him.... runes.

These were more than mere alphabets. Each rune was a symbol containing innate magic, and if used in the right manner, these runes were able to weave magic unlike any.

Odin screams with ecstasy and pain as this knowledge is revealed to him and falls from the tree. His sacrifice has not been for naught. After all, he has just learned the greatest source of magic in the entire universe. Runes.

What You Will Learn In This Book

A large part of this book pertains to runes, and another significant part revolves around Norse magic. However, there's so much more to Norse mythology and magic than just runes and rituals. I'd love to get into all of that with you, primarily:

- How the world of Norse Mythology came into being.
- The Nine Realms of Norse Mythology and the beings that reside in them.
- The Norse Pantheon, including the Æsir and Vanir gods.
- The A-List gods of Norse Mythology, such as Odin, Thor, and Freya.
- An introduction to Norse Paganism.
- A divination of runes.
- The fascinating world of Norse Magic.
- Practicing Norse Magic in our daily lives through different rituals such as Blót and Sumbel.

A Little About Me

Norse Mythology, magic, runes, gods, and goddesses have played a crucial role in my life. Growing up in Kungsträdgården, Sweden, the stories of the gods and goddesses served as a whetstone to the proverbial blade of my imagination. I'd spend days upon days dreaming about the gods and goddesses and doing hilarious cosplays, such as dressing up as Freya and tying a makeshift chariot to my cats.

For me, though, these were more than just folkloric stories. These were the tales of my ancestors. My forefathers believed in these deities and performed these rituals. This realization led me down a rabbit hole of discovery through reading and researching every source I could get my hands on to uncover as much as I could about Norse culture.

Although I was raised Christian, I could never connect with the religion and always felt disconcerted by its beliefs, believing that many of them were forced and contrived. This divide between me and divinity made me dig deeper into my past. That's when I discovered that my ancestors were followers of the old Norse religion. The more I learned about their beliefs, the more I felt them align with my own innate beliefs until a moment of clarity came, and it all clicked into place.

After devoting my time to learning about Norse Mythology and culture, I delved deep into modern practices such as Ásatrú, adopting them into my daily life by performing divination and rituals. The fulfillment and satisfaction that I found in reconnecting with the gods and goddesses and the spirits of my ancestors through these profound practices were second to none.

Why You Should Read This Book

And to you, I extend the same invitation that you rediscover the secrets that were once lost. That you learn about runes, magic, rituals, and beliefs that will transform your life, I can provide you with the framework and tools required to make this journey and initiate you to the old Norse ways.

- If at any time you have felt like you don't know where to begin and how to find your footing in this vast universe, I am here to show you where to start.
- If you're craving deeper knowledge about Norse Mythology after coming across the gods and goddesses in modern media such as video games (God of War, Hellblade, Assassin's Creed), movies (Thor), TV shows (Vikings), and books (American Gods), or any other media, it would be my privilege to share a more mystical and deeper perspective on your favorite icons from Norse mythology such as Loki, Odin, and Thor.
- If you're a keen learner of history, cultures, and religions, then we are well met. There's nothing more amazing than coming across fellow nerds who desire a deep dive into this wondrous topic.
- You may be interested in finding out more about Norse Mythology and its associated rites and rituals after you've taken a DNA test and have discovered that you're related to the Vikings and want to know more about your history.
- If you have felt a calling to the old ways through inexplicable signs, dreams, and visions, or if you've felt drawn to the wisdom of the gods and goddesses and are wondering what it all means, then consider this yet another sign, for you're headed in the right direction. Allow me to be a humble guide in your journey and share some

valuable insights with you that may serve to strengthen your connection with your roots and allow you to connect with the gods through divine rituals.

- Lastly, if you're looking for a reliable source of genuine information on Norse Mythology, let's say, for a school project or a dissertation, then you can use my works as a reference to help you.

Through this book, I aim to teach you about the different forms of magic and divination, give you a solid understanding of who the gods and goddesses were and what domains they held power over, how we prayed to them in the past, and how we can do so in our daily lives now, what modern ceremonies and rituals are being followed by pagans all over the world and how they're connected to the gods and goddesses, and most importantly, how rune magic works.

I hope you're as brimming with excitement and intrigue as I am, for we're going to delve into such rich history and explore such fertile territory of runes, magic, and rituals, that by the time you're finished reading this book, you can confidently say that you're an authority on all these matters.

CHAPTER 1
THE NORDIC BIG BANG — BEGINNING OF NORSE MYTHOLOGY

On the Nature of Myths

Every culture of significance comes with its assorted myths and legends. Some of these are more than just stories and are meant to explain how the world works. A Hindu cleric might have noticed that the night sky resembled a flowing river and concluded that the Ganga flowed down on the earth from the cosmos and that the earth was cradled between the horns of a celestial cow. Abrahamic religions fathomed that the world, which came into being all of a sudden, did so because of the word of God. The Greeks held similar beliefs about the world, believing that Gaia and other divine beings such as Eros, Abyss, and Erebus came from the unending Chaos.

Myths, fables, and legends serve another core function by offering a rational (or rational adjacent) explanation to an otherwise chaotic world. While in other instances, they record such events that are so monumental that they deserve a place in the annals of history. These stories about the supernatural or inexplicable weave themselves into the thread of history and form our current understanding of history.

To that end, there are three types of stories that preserve events or describe phenomena, namely myth, legends, and folklore.

Myths

Myths tackle the big picture stuff, asking questions like where did we come from, how the world came into being, and who granted us the ability to create fire or speak in different languages. But more relevantly, myths concern divinity. They try to unravel the mystery of gods and goddesses and lend credence to their existence through stories.

Because of the diverse range of topics that myths cover, they have generally been categorized into three types:

- **Psychological Myths**
- **Historical Myths**
- **Etiological Myths**

Psychological myths detail journeys that start from the known and end in the unknown such as Oedipus's tale, who travels far away to avoid the prediction that he'll end up killing his father. In this new land, he ends up killing a man who was his father and who had similarly abandoned the same land because he, too, wanted to prevent the prophecy from coming true. The psychological nature of this myth contains a moral lesson that it is futile to avoid your fate as decreed by the gods.

Historical myths retell actual events and elevate them by restructuring the narrative in a grandiose manner. The siege of Troy is described in Homer's Iliad in a reframed way, changing the nature of the story from being factual to being a historical myth.

Etiological myths are concerned with explaining how something came to be or why it is the way it is. Origin stories, in other terms. Thunder, for example, according to etiological myths, is the sound of Thor's chariot racing across the sky. In etiological myths, characters tend to serve a purpose that aligns their role with the story's actions or consequences. In Chinese mythology, Nuwa, the goddess, upon growing tired of creating humans over and over again, decided to call it quits and introduce the practice of marriage so that humans could reproduce on their own.

Perhaps one of the best-known etiological myths is the story of Demeter and her daughter, Persephone. Persephone gets kidnapped by the god of the underworld, Hades. Demeter, who was the goddess of grain and harvest, became so sorrowful at being apart from her daughter that all the crops started failing, and people began starving. Zeus ordered Hades to return Persephone to her mother. However, Persephone, having eaten some of the pomegranate seeds from the underworld, has to spend half of the year under the earth but could come back to the earth for the other half.

Besides telling this epic where Demeter's sorrow moved the gods to interfere with Hades to return Persephone, this myth also tries to explain why seasons changed the way they did in Greece back then. When the weather was warm, and the fields were full, Persephone was assumed to be united with her mom. When it was cold and dark, and barren, people assumed that Persephone was biding her time in the underworld and her mom was mourning.

Legends

Legends are a little more grounded when it comes to the subject matter, dealing not with gods and divinity as much as they do with tales of heroes who perform feats of nobility, courage, and bravery. Legends of people like Ragnar Lothbrok, Robin Hood, and King Arthur have an element of fantasy to them where the stories are sometimes inflated in their magnitude as they pass through generations.

Folklore

Folklores are stories that depict beliefs and convictions, especially those that are confined to a particular region. Fairies in England, the Loch Ness monster in Scotland, Draugrs in Scandinavia, and Djinns in Arabia are all examples of folklore. Some of these folkloric tales are rooted in superstition whilst others are contorted versions of the truth. Regardless of their origin, these serve to entertain and educate people with moralistic values often tethered to them.

Norse Mythology embodies all three types of tales. The great fables of Odin and Thor are examples of myths preserved by historians like Snorri Sturluson. Legends of Erik the Red and Ragnar Lothbrok are instances where the mythology doesn't just rely on gods and goddesses but focuses on the mortal side as well. And folklore about mystical creatures like Huldra and Fossegrim shows us that Norse Mythology is rich with its fair share of folk tales.

The pre-Christian religion, beliefs, legends, and myths of the Scandinavian and Icelandic people are the primary source of Norse Mythology, with many of these stories being shared and propagated by the Northern Germanic tribes of the 9th century. Most of these stories were passed down in the form of poems, songs, and ballads until they were compiled in the form of Eddas and medieval texts between the 11th and 18th centuries.

As with all tales that stand the test of time, the very best of them were compiled and preserved in the Poetic and Prose Edda, which are considered two of the chief references of Norse Mythology.

The old gods took measures to make sure their tales survived time, invasion, and missionaries from other religions. The very air of Scandinavia can attest to that. Even if there were no sources left, the names of old towns and cities would remain, many of which are named after Norse deities. And say, if you will, that even those cease to exist, then the runic inscriptions spread throughout Scandinavia will attest to the existence of the gods. Besides runic inscriptions, a lot of imagery still survives from the old days, depicting scenes such as Thor's fishing trip and Odin being devoured by Fenrir. Many figurines from that era have survived, showing Thor, Freyr, and Odin.

So long as there are devout followers of the Old Norse Religion, and so long as there are reliable sources that have resiliently stood the test of time, we do not have to worry about this great culture losing itself to oblivion. Not while there are kindred spirits such as you and me. The great news I have for you is this: We are an ever-growing movement. Every day, more people are finding their ancient roots and reconnecting with Norse Mythology and its practices through modern paganism sects like Ásatrú, Vanatru, Rokkatru, Heathenism, Lokeans, and so much more. Many New Age movements and recent belief systems, such as Wicca, Witchcraft, and Shamanism, have also adopted various aspects of Norse Mythology.

I can assure you we're only going to keep growing.

The more accessible our modern world has become, the more it has allowed people to get their hands on information that was previously obscure or purposefully kept hidden from them. Not so long ago, there was a time when the Christianization of Europe declared all paganistic elements to be blasphemous. Witches were burnt, heretics were hung, and blasphemers were banished. But that was then, and this is now. Now is our time.

With the internet, social media, and online forums, we have found others like us and formed online and IRL communities, communities that have enabled us to rebirth the ancient religion in new forms.

I can only say that we're living in exciting times where we're getting to witness this rebirth in real-time. It's almost cyclical in nature, much like Norse cosmology, where the end is not an end but a new beginning.

So let's begin anew this tale of cosmic creation and discuss the origin of Norse Mythology itself.

The Beginning, Before, and After

Before there was anything, there was the endless space, the gap known as Ginnungagap, which in Old Norse meant gaping abyss. This is where the Norse creation myth begins.

In the North of that gap was a well known as the Hvergelmir. The great World Tree, Yggdrasil, drew water from this well.

As it happened, the north of the Ginnungagap was intensely cold. Whatever water was not consumed by the Yggdrasil fled up north, where it froze and eventually formed the icy world of Niffelheim.

Ginnungagap's south was as hot as its north was cold. As it grew hotter, the fiery region started to form a realm that was the polar opposite of Niffelheim. This came to be known as Muspelheim, the realm of fire and blaze.

Amidst the endless nothing of the cosmos, something started happening that would serve as the prelude to the world as we know it. The heat from Muspelheim slowly started reaching the cold recesses of Niffelheim, eventually thawing some of the ice and causing water droplets to descend to Muspelheim, where when they came into contact with the fire, they caused sparks.

As this process perpetuated, more water fell on the billowing flames and caused steam and mist to emanate and concentrate until finally, it took shape of the first sentient being, Ymir, the giant. Who knows for how long all that flame and mist and steam must have infused until it became cognizant enough and formed a body?

Ymir, otherwise known as the Screamer, was hermaphroditic, reproducing asexually. When this giant slept, more giants birthed from his legs and the warm sweat of his armpits.

But Ymir and his children weren't the only beings to come forth at this early stage. As the frost melted, a cow, Auðumbla, named so because she hummed in abundance, emerged. This cow had a maternal inclination; she nourished Ymir with her milk. As for her own nutrition, she licked the salt atop the icy rocks of Niffelheim. Through her continued licking, the ice started taking shape. Eventually, the ice took the shape of Buri, the first god.

Buri then had a child named Borr. Though, how he did that is shrouded in mystery. Buri also had a daughter named Bestla, whom Borr married. In other lore, Bestla was one of the first Jötnar who were formed from Ymir's sweat.

Borr and Bestla became parents to three sons, Odin, Vili, and Ve.

The three brothers saw the cruelty of Ymir and his children. In some cases, they even experienced it firsthand. Ymir was chaotic, hoarding, and violent. If Ymir was the epitome of unrealized potential and chaos, the brothers were the opposite. They realized their powers, tapped into them, and plotted to kill Ymir.

They succeeded in killing Ymir. It was only after taking the first giant's life that the brothers found themselves thrust into the process of creation.

A note here. What do Ymir and the Ginnungagap depict, if not chaos and the state of rawness before creation? The Ginnungagap was unending and limitless in its potential, but all of that potential was unrealized for the longest time. Similarly, Ymir, rather than seeking an order or choosing to become an active participant in the process of creation, through his nature, opted to be a source of violence and havoc. The gods, as soon as they came into being, realized their potential, sought order, and did what they could to give the chaotic world around them some semblance of form.

After they killed Ymir, rivers of blood flowed from the dead giant's body, flowing away most of Ymir's children. Those who remained became the progenitors of the Jötnar. Ymir's body hung suspended in the center of the Ginnungagap.

The brothers saw the corpse and realized what had to be done. They had to create something out of this humungous dead body. They formed the surface of the world with his body and used his blood to make bodies of water such as rivers and seas. His bones and teeth were erected to create the mountains and fjords. The gods were very resourceful in their creative process, not letting any part of Ymir go to waste.

From his skull, they created the sky dome and used his brains as clouds. Odin and his brothers captured the sparks flying from Muspelheim and placed them in the sky to serve the purpose of stars, the moon, and the sun.

The gods, having experienced chaos, knew the challenge it posed and how the beings of chaos, the Jötnar, could possibly cause turbulence to the lives of those who would live on this new world. As a precautionary measure, they took the eyebrows of the dead giant and built a wall around this land to keep it secure.

They dubbed this world Midgard, calling it so because of Yggdrasil's frame of reference and Midgard's relative position to it.

Once they were satisfied with the world they had created, they began creating the beings who would reside in this world. They took tree branches and carved them in the shape of a man and woman and imbued them with life. The man and woman were named Ask and Embla and were sent forth into Midgard to live and propagate the race of humanity.

Around this time, new worlds also formed. One such world, called Asgard, became the home of Odin and his kin. Jötunnheim became home to the Jötunn. Other beings nestled in other realms, such as the dwarves in Svartalfheim and the elves in Alfheim.

During the process of Midgard's creation, worms kept crawling out of Ymir's rotting body. Eventually, these worms evolved into dwarves. Odin, Vili, and Ve noticed that the sky would fall if it were not held up at all times. To take care of its precarious nature, they designated four dwarves to hold up the sky. Each dwarf was sent in each direction. Nordi to North, Vestri to West, Sundri to South, and Austri to East. The remaining dwarves who were not given such duties made their home in the rocks and caverns of Svartalfheim, where, through the refinement of their craft, they became masters of forgery and smithery, creating such powerful weapons as Mjolnir, Thor's hammer.

We will get to see these worlds, the beings that thrive in them, and how these worlds shape the history, present, and future of Norse mythology. A few of these worlds will also play a key role in Ragnarök.

Norse Mythology In Our Modern World

There's no doubt about it that Norse Mythology is enjoying a very three-dimensional renaissance in our popular culture, from novels like *The Gospel of Loki* becoming bestsellers to video games like *God of War: Ragnarök* stealing the show at The Game Awards 2022. And who can forget the box-office hit *Thor* movies that introduced us to a whimsical version of Norse Mythology as imagined by Marvel?

Modern video games with hyperrealism and photorealism have created jaw-dropping spectacles where playing each game—*God of War, Assassin's Creed: Valhalla, Hellblade*—feels not like playing a childish game but instead going on a digital pilgrimage across these beautifully recreated lands. As Kratos in *God of War*, you journey through the Nine Realms, come face to face with central figures, and play a key role in the events that shaped Norse Mythology. As an Assassin in *Assassin's Creed*, you don the garb of a Viking as you go on expeditions across England, truly putting yourself in the shoes of those fierce warriors. In *Hellblade*, you get to witness the brutal and raw nature of the Vikings and Scandinavia from a Celtic perspective, descending into Helheim itself and coming across Hela.

There's something for everyone's palettes, for if someone wants a more nuanced approach to the tales of old, there's always *Vikings* by History Channel, which shows the mythos for what it truly is—often bleak, unforgiving, and brutal—and instead of myths, focuses on legends and tells the stories of famous Viking figures such as Ragnar Lothbrok and Erik the Red. There is an entire ecosystem of Norse channels on YouTube where people nerd out about the Vikings, the Norse deities, and ancient Nordic practices reimagined and repurposed for the 21st century.

And I do mean three-dimensional. It's not just pop-culture that has been infused with Norse Mythology, providing us spectacles like Neil Gaiman's *American Gods* and mental-health-oriented games like *Hellblade: Senua's Sacrifice*; Norse Mythology has been resuscitated in a religious and cultural form as well. For thousands of people, it's more than just entertainment; it's a way of life. For thousands of others, it's a way to reconnect with their long-lost roots. Paganistic sects with ties to the Old Norse religion have proudly hoisted their colors in different forms, such as Ásatrú, Vanatru, Heathenry, Shamanism, and Wicca.

Those who practice Norse Paganism have delved beyond the superficial adaptations and have truly embraced that lifestyle by performing runic magic, creating altars for worship and invocation, aligning themselves with the Norse beliefs, and celebrating the holidays of the Norse calendar. I aim to provide you with the necessary background information first and then introduce you to the rituals, runes, and rites that will allow you to become a profound partaker in the subtler and deeper aspects of Norse Mythology.

With that in mind, we're going to learn more about the Nine Realms in the upcoming chapter and then learn about the various deities and beings that reside in those realms.

CHAPTER 2
THE NINE REALMS

Norse Cosmology has ten important locations that are central to the stories, the adventures of the gods, and the conflict that will eventually cause Ragnarök .

There is a bit of prejudice in historical accounts when writing about the realms as most of the descriptions and stories concern Midgard, it being the home to our race and the only world that we as humans were most familiar with.

These ten locations include:

- Yggdrasil — the World Tree which nestles all the realms.
- Asgard — Realm of the Æsir gods, joined to Midgard through the Bifrost.
- Alfheim — Where the elves dwelled.
- Vanaheim — Realm of the Vanir gods.
- Svartalfheim — Realm of the dwarves.

- Muspelheim — The realm of fire, where Surtr, the fire giant, lived and nourished his forces of chaos.
- Niffelheim — A place of ice, snow, cold, and mist.
- Helheim — A realm where those who died of natural causes, illnesses, and old age went. It's also where Hel, the goddess of the underworld, lives.
- Midgard — Our realm, the realm of human beings.
- Jötunnheim — The land of frost giants, the Jötnar.

Yggdrasil

The great eternal ash tree stands in the center of the universe, its branches stretching out all across the cosmos, cradling the Nine Realms within it. Each Realm has its branch. All life depends upon this tree, as any harm to the Yggdrasil would destroy all realms.

We discussed this tree in the beginning when we read about Odin's journey to divine runes. Yggdrasil is vast, with three giant roots extending deep below. Each root has a well alongside it to nourish it with water and nutrients. The first root is uncannily deep, reaching below Niffelheim, where the realm of Helheim is situated. The first root has a well known as Hvergelmir, also known as the Well of Poison, and yet, this is the same well from where the water rose at the beginning that turned to mist and steam and formed Ymir.

A great dragon by the name of Níðhöggr is trapped under the first root, harming it every moment by chewing on it. On Ragnarök, the dragon will succeed in breaking free from the root and cause havoc hitherto undreamt of.

The second root is in the land of frost giants, besides a well known as Mimir's well, also known as The Well of Wisdom. Mimir drinks from this well and attains wisdom from it. Sometimes, he lets other beings drink from it as well, but at the cost of a heavy sacrifice. When Odin wanted to drink from this well, Mimir asked him to sacrifice something, in response to which Odin tore out his eye and flung it into the water.

The third root is in Asgard and has a well known as the Well of Urd, where the Norns—masters of fate and the personification of destiny and time—reside. The Norns collect water from the well and pour it over Yggdrasil to sustain it. If they stop doing so, the tree will rot.

Yggdrasil has many denizens, such as the mischievous squirrel called Ratatoskr and the elusive eagle who sits atop the tree. The tree has a very protective and paternal role. At Ragnarök, the last two human beings will find shelter inside the tree and will remain within its sanctuary until the end is over, and it's safe to go out.

Asgard

There are few realms in mythologies in general as resplendent as Asgard. Olympus comes to mind, but even Olympus was not as humungous in size as to span an entire cosmic body that the gods called home. For you to understand the sheer scale of Asgard, I'll tell you this: There are dozens of realms within Asgard's walls that are ecosystems of their own such as Valhalla or Fólkvangr, where the Valkyries escort those who died valiantly.

Besides being massive, Asgard is the pinnacle of luxury and magnificence. It is, after all, the land of the Æsir gods. Of the Nine Realms, the only two Realms that have been written prolifically about are Midgard and Asgard.

Odin rules Asgard, holding dominion over other Æsir gods and the brave souls of the martyrs, also known as the einherjar. Complete with castles, throne-rooms, armories, banquet halls, and courtyards, it was a kingdom of plenty, with fortifications barring it from the rest of the world, a magical bridge connecting it to other lands, and vast fields, lush forests, deep rivers, towering mountains, grand fjords, and tumultuous oceans giving it a geographical diversity.

Its halls had hundreds of rooms, its lands were expansive and everywhere in the realm, and the air was vibrant with magic. One of these massive halls with more than five hundred rooms was Valhalla, where the fallen warriors reveled in endless feasts and engaged in sportsmanly displays of fights. Flames roared in fireplaces, and massive boars were roasted for these warriors, also known as the einherjar. They would drink mead and regale each other with tales of their battles on Earth. They'd be reunited with their forefathers in this hall, this hall made of shields and spears.

Another regal location within Asgard was Hliðskjálf, the palace of Odin, where from his throne, he could see into every realm. Other gods had similar halls as well, such as Bilskirnir, Thor's hall, which was said to be one of the grandest halls in Valhalla. Thor had his own land there, too, known as Thrudheim. Freya, another notable goddess, had a field where she'd bring the spirits of the fallen warriors. This field was called Fólkvangr. Baldur, another Æsir god, had a home in Asgard known as Breiðablik, a place so pure and clean that no evil thing could exist within it. Heimdall, a chief god, had a home called Himinbjörg near the border of Asgard near the Bifrost, from where he could watch over all things.

Alfheim

A place of light, beauty, glamour, and radiance, Alfheim was home to the elves. They were described as beings more beautiful than the sun, and their world was a just reflection of its residents.

Alfheim is said to have been ruled by Freyr, the god of fertility, virility, and prosperity. Freyr was originally a Vanir god and was given the realm of Alfheim as a tooth gift, a gift given to infants when they broke their first tooth.

There's a deep relationship between the Vanir gods and nature. While the Æsir gods have more political, physical, and magical strength, the Vanir gods make use of their connection with nature to foster natural growth, fertility, and harmony with all living things. That Freyr was given Alfheim as a gift tells us that Alfheim and its residents must also have been kindred spirits with the Vanir when it came to a respectful relationship with nature.

The Eddas and other surviving texts do not go into great detail about Alfheim, primarily because the elves and Alfheim, as such, do not have much of a narrative role to play in the stories and myths of Norse Mythology. But this has not stopped others to draw inspiration from the

Alfheim elves and their native land, as many authors, especially those of Indo-European literature, reimagined elves and introduced them in their own books. Tolkien comes to mind, with his version of elves and their lands, such as Rivendell, depicting the same resplendence as the source of their inspiration.

The elves who resided in Alfheim were beautiful, intelligent, magical, and had an inclination towards music, arts, and other forms of creativity.

The geographical inspiration for Alfheim was the land between Sweden and Norway between the rivers Gota and Glom, a place that was quite beautiful and bright as compared to the rest of Scandinavia and whose people appeared fairer and more artistic. However, this is just a scholarly claim, and it is not entirely a well-rooted claim at that.

Vanaheim

Home to the Vanir gods, this Realm was a counterpart to Asgard and was the birthplace of Njord, who was the patriarch of the Vanir.

Unfortunately, most of the descriptions in the Eddas are about Midgard and Asgard and shed little light on the other realms, but there are still some scant details mentioned that allow us to learn more about this world.

Even though there isn't much written about Vanaheim or the gods living therein, the Norse people revered the Vanir gods because of their prowess when it came to nature, land, fertility, and holistic magic. In fact, the major war between the Vanir and Æsir took place because of this reason. The Vanir were much more loved by the people and received more sacrifices and offerings as a result.

Even though battle and warfare were the specialties of the Æsir gods, the Vanirs held their own in that war, and eventually, after much bloodshed, the two sides came to a truce. Njord, Freyr, and Freya, three Vanir gods, were sent to live with the Æsir, and Mimir and Hoenir, two Æsir gods, were sent to Vanaheim as part of this barter.

Because of the truce, the gods from both groups were considered equals and would receive an equal amount of honor and sacrifice from the humans.

The underlying reason why the Vanir were, before the war, much more beloved to the humans was because of the powers that fell within their purview. Freya and Freyr were both deities related to the fertility of different types—humans, animals, and crops. Njord was related to the sea, which the Norse people had to rely on for both travel and food. While worshiping the Æsir helped humans in matters such as government, warfare, might, intelligence, and politics, worshipping the Vanir meant prosperity in terms of fertility, peace, happiness, and affluence.

Besides Freya, Freyr, and Njord, some other Vanir deities included Gersemi, Hnoss, Gullveig, and Kvasir.

Lastly, the stark difference between the residents of Vanaheim and Asgard was their perspective on rules. Among the main reasons for the war between the Æsir and Vanir, besides the worship bias, was their opposing view on rules. The Æsir believed that humans should follow strict rules and structure, while the Vanir were more lenient.

One such example of this was the marriage between siblings. While the Æsir completely forbade such an act, the Vanir often married among siblings. Njord was married to his sister. The two had Freya and Freyr. We will discuss more the Æsir and Vanir in the upcoming chapter about the Norse pantheon.

Jötunheimr / Jötunheimar/ Jötunnheim

The land of the giants was a cold, desolate, rugged, and mountainous region, with its residents being hostile to outsiders, especially the gods. There was a rivalry between the gods and the giants from the beginning, and the giants remembered this.

Throughout the accounts and Eddas, the giants are described as chaotic beings of violence and malice. This has been mentioned so many times that one cannot help but wonder if the authors were biased in favor of the gods. As Norse mythology has often shown us time and again, there's no such thing as black or white in that world. Evil is not entirely evil, and good is not necessarily good. Loki, often seen as a similar agent of chaos, has redeemed himself many times by doing the right thing. Thor, on the other hand, dubbed good and brave and a friend of humans has sometimes gone out to hunt and kill giants as a sport.

Jötunnheim was the place where the giants took shelter after Ymir was killed, and his blood wiped away most of his offspring. The remaining giants having good reason to hate the gods for killing their ancestors.

The Eddas describe this land as bleak. There is constant darkness looming on the horizon. The forests are deep and dark. The mountains are unconquerable and jagged. There is no fertility here. The giants adapted to this harsh climate by hunting and fishing.

Another important aspect of this land is the river Iving that separates Jötunnheim from Midgard and Asgard. This river never freezes and thus prevents the giants from crossing over to those other realms.

Jötunnheim was also known as Utgard, which translated to "world beyond the fence." Unlike the ordered structure and norms found in Asgard and Midgard, lawlessness and chaos prevailed in Jötunnheim.

Some of the most prominent residents of Jötunnheim include Skadi, Gerd, Jarnsaxa, Bestla, Grid, Rindr, Gunnlod, Hrod, Jord, and Sigyn.

One last interesting bit of trivia about Jötunnheim is that when Thor visits the stronghold of the giant Utgard-Loki, he is told that nothing that Thor will experience on his journey is what it appears to be and that nothing is to be trusted.

Svartalfheim

The dwarves of Norse mythology are very goal-oriented, single-minded, and driven. These characteristics have enabled them to become masters of their smithing craft. The only two times that Svartalfheim is mentioned in the Eddas are related to the craft of the dwarves.

In the first tale, the gods go to the realm to find chains that will be powerful enough to hold a monolithic wolf known as Fenrir. In the second tale, Loki travels to the realm to find Andvari and seize his gold.

The gods rely upon the dwarves in many ways. When Midgard was made, Odin and his brothers sent forth four dwarves in each direction to hold the sky aloft. Because of their craftsmanship, the gods have come to the dwarves time and again for powerful weapons and artifacts. The dwarves made Thor's hammer and Odin's spear. They even built a magic ship for Freyr. The Mead of Poetry is also the creation of the dwarves.

Unlike Jötunnheim, Svartaflheim is not grim. It is dark, sure, and it has many caverns, caves, mines, and forges, but it is not without its share of warmth and homeliness. The dwarves live in the caves, mine in them, and make weapons in them. Call to mind the Mines of Moria from *Lord of the Rings.*

In one of the famous tales written in the Edda, Loki cuts off Thor's wife's hair. Thor seizes Loki and is about to break every bone in his body when Loki says that he's going to make everything all right by traveling to Svartalfheim.

Loki then goes to the realm and seeks out the dwarves. He asks them to make golden hair for Sif. But Loki does not want to stop there. He also commissions them to make an unsinkable ship and a deadly spear.

Loki being Loki, a master of mischief and cunning, finds the two best metalsmiths in the realm and then taunts them that they cannot craft anything as awesome as the items he already possesses. The brothers take the bait and make him a golden-haired boar that glows in the dark and runs through air and water, and can travel faster than any horse. They also make him a golden ring that sprouts eight identical rings every ninth night, and, of course, Mjolnir.

When he returns to Asgard, he gives the golden hair to Sif and the hammer to Thor. One can only suspect that Loki robbed Sif of her original hair for a chance to go to Svartalfheim and get the dwarves to make all these magical artifacts and weapons for him.

Muspelheim

This primeval world of fire was the source and catalyst for creation, along with the other elemental world, Niffelheim. The flames from Muspelheim caused mist and steam to rise after some water from Niffelheim dropped on it, thus creating Ymir and Auðumbla.

This realm will also play a key role in the destruction of the world. Just as the fire from this realm once made Ymir's existence possible, so too will its fires cause the annihilation of the world during Ragnarök .

The fire-giant Surtr will rise from this realm and use his flaming sword to burn the world and kill the gods.

The realm of fire was so remote and dangerous that few seldom ventured there. Besides fiery chasms of flame and magma, there is a vanguard of fire giants commanded by Surtr waiting for his command. When Surtr will rise, he will command his vanguard to go forth and take the fire of Muspelheim with them and destroy the entire world.

Surtr will face off in battle with Freyr. Freyr, who will have given his trusty sword to his servant, will be left relatively compromised and will die in this battle. The last thing the world will know before its death will be Muspelheim's flames.

There is a poetic irony here that Norse mythology starts with ice and flame and ends with ice and flame. It further embeds the notion of the cyclical nature of reality deeper in the belief system of those who follow Norse paganism.

Muspelheim and Niffelheim are considered cosmic constants that control the fate of the world through their continuous existence. After the world will end as a result of Ragnarök, it will begin anew in a similar fashion to how it began once. Because of the chaos it represented and because of its sheer primordiality, it was respected and feared by the Norse people.

Niffelheim

Niffelheim literally means the world of fog. One of the two primeval worlds, this world is the polar opposite of Muspelheim and is host to darkness, cold, mist, ice, and frost. It was because of this realm that Buri, the first of the gods, came into existence after Auðumbla kept licking the ice for her nourishment.

In so many accounts, the world of Niffelheim is often used synonymously with Helheim. There are differences in the accounts, leading to some scholars claiming that both realms were the same and other scholars saying that they were two different lands.

Snorri Sturluson, the author of the Poetic Edda, claimed that most terrible things emerged from Niffelheim, hinting that the world was not just primordial but also a place of evil.

Midgard

Midgard's name suggests that its position was in the center of all the nine realms, cradling it in such a way that the holier worlds of Asgard, Alfheim, and Vanaheim were above it while the drearier lands like Jötunnheim and Hel were below it.

We have already looked at Midgard's creation and the subsequent population at length in the previous chapter.

It is said that the gods feared the offspring of Loki and Angrboða as Odin divined to them that they are going to be the harbingers of Ragnarök. So, as a precautionary measure, the gods separated the siblings. One of these children was the colossal serpent Jörmungandr. The gods flung him into the ocean that surrounded Midgard. Here, the serpent grew and grew until it was humungous enough to envelop the entire world by coiling around it and putting his tail in his mouth.

Thor is often depicted as an ally to Midgard and a friend to its people. He would visit the people often and have a jolly good time.

Upon Ragnarök, the sun and moon will disappear from Midgard's sky, and the earth will start shaking fiercely, causing the trees to topple and the mountains to fall. Jörmungandr will emerge from the water and throw venom in every direction. When he gets out, he'll cause giant waves to drown the realm, eventually destroying it as a result of his battle with Thor.

Helheim

People often mistake the Christian version of Hell for Helheim based on the similar name, but Helheim means "house of Hel" and has no resemblance to the infernal Abrahamic hell.

One of the Nine Realms, this place serves as the afterlife abode for souls who died of old age, natural causes, or disease.

Just as Jörmungandr was thrown to Midgard and Fenrir was chained, Hel, the daughter of Loki, was banished to this realm to avert Ragnarök for as long as possible. Hel is described to be half black and half flesh-colored, showing that she's half dead and half alive. Hel quickly took command of this realm and attained dominion over the souls of the dead.

Hel was not exactly bound in Helheim. She was free to move within her realm as she pleased and even had a home under Yggdrasil's branches. While Helheim didn't exactly have burning pyres of lava pits, it was still a dreadful place because of the cold, fog, and darkness. This was not intentional. It was just the nature of this place. Hel tried to make the people who came here as comfortable as possible, often giving them gifts and lodging in an attempt to provide them some small comfort.

Once a soul traversed to Hel, it could not come back. One of the most popular instances of this is when Baldur, the beloved god of the Æsir, died because of Loki's trickery. Hermod volunteered to go to Hel on Frigg's behalf. Odin lent him his steed, Sleipnir, and even on that steed, it took nine nights for Hermod to travel between the realms. Hermod saw that Baldur was being treated quite honorably in Hel. He asked Hel if he could take him back. Hel said that if everything in the world would weep for him, she'd consider sending him back.

Hermod went back to Asgard and told the gods of this. The gods spread the word throughout the Nine Realms, asking every creature to weep for Baldur. Everyone cried, except for Thokk, an old giantess who said that she had no love for Odin and his kin and she'd rather let Baldur stay in Hel then mourn him. Some sources claim that Thokk was Loki in disguise.

Because the wager was not fulfilled, Baldur had to stay in Hel indefinitely.

Before Ragnarök, Hel will rise from Helheim with her horde of the dead. Jörmungandr will emerge from the sea. Fenrir will break free from his chains. A battle like none other will take place where Loki will command the armies of the dead, eventually causing the end of the world.

Other notable creatures residing within Hel include the dragon Níðhöggr, the guard-dog Garm, and a Völva whom Odin used to receive prophecies of Ragnarök.

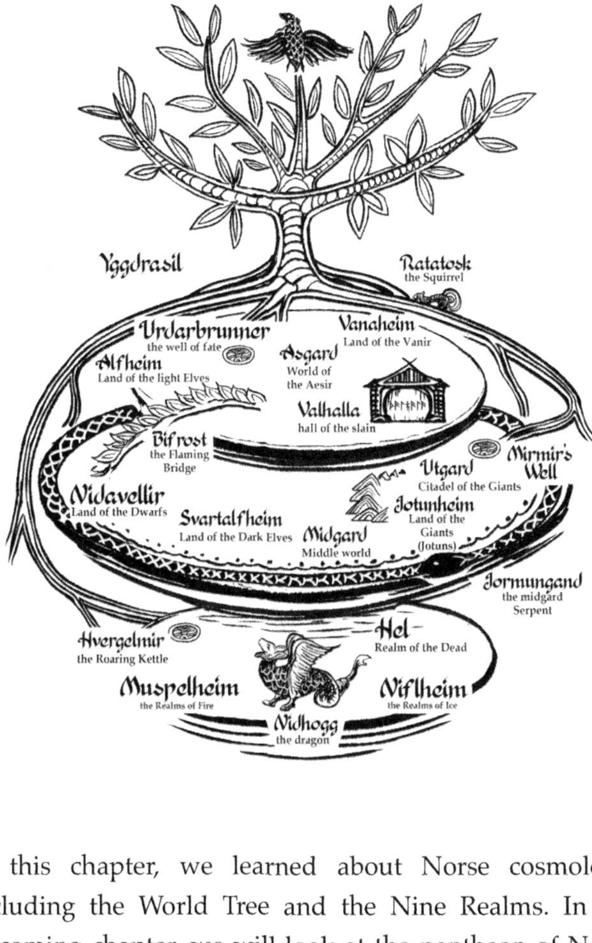

In this chapter, we learned about Norse cosmology, including the World Tree and the Nine Realms. In the upcoming chapter, we will look at the pantheon of Norse Mythology and shed light on the two main clans of gods, the Æsir and the Vanir. After that, we're going to look at their abilities and their distinguishing features. The reason this information is important is that it gives us insight into how different magics, rituals, and rites work concerning different deities.

CHAPTER 3
THE PANTHEON OF NORSE MYTHOLOGY

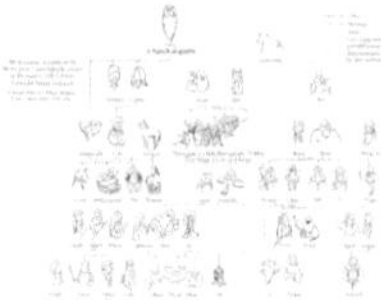

Before the Eddas and other such volumes were compiled somewhere between the 11th and 18th centuries, the stories that we now know as Norse Mythology were passed down in the form of poetry. Often, these tales were told around the fire, much in a folkloric sense, and just as often, these tales were told to the children by their parents to instill the importance of their culture from an early age.

The old Norse religion and the assorted myths came from the Northern Germanic tribes of the 9th AD. Before Christianity became prevalent through missionary work, the Scandinavian people, including the Icelandic folk, adhered to the old Norse religion. The Norse Mythology we know of today comes from figures and stories derived from multiple sources, including medieval scripts, archeological evidence, and folklore. It is a descendant of the Indo-European religion of the late Neolithic period.

The gods and goddesses they worshipped were divided into two main categories, the Æsir and the Vanir. Most of what we know about these deities comes from Snorri Sturluson's Prose Edda and Poetic Edda.

The Æsir Gods

Descendants of Buri, the first god, the Æsir gods embodied power, warfare, might, politics, and strength. They were known for their physical traits and their military tactics as compared to the Vanir, who had more of a natural disposition. There are more significant differences between the two groups, including their values. While the Æsir are more concerned with how the humans who worship them should be more adherent to rules and order, the Vanir believe that humans should be granted leniency and should do as they please. The Æsir valued strength and battle tactics, while the Vanir valued nature, harmony with one's surroundings, and mysticism.

The term Æsir comes from ansaz, which means beam or pole, or ansuz, which means life or vitality.

They were natives of Asgard and, with their collective governance under Odin, were able to hold dominion over the cosmos for a certain period. Unlike deities from other mythologies, the Æsir were not entirely immortal. They had to consume golden apples from Iðunn's tree to maintain their immortality and their strength. Even according to the lore, the gods were destined to die at Ragnarök, creating a stark difference between Norse gods and gods from other religions.

They are worshipped to this day, especially by neo-paganism sects like Ásatrú, which was built upon the polytheistic foundation of the old Norse religion.

While we're only going through the names of the gods and goddesses for now, we're going to take a deeper look at the A-list of Norse deities in the next chapter. Some of the most prominent Æsir gods include:

Odin

The chief of the Æsir, Odin, was known for his love for knowledge and his quests for wisdom. He had sacrificed so much in his journey to attain the truth. Besides being an ardent pursuer of knowledge, Odin was a god of war and held dominion over battlefields.

Because of his many salient attributes, he is considered the patron deity of poets, slain warriors, kings, and courageous men. He oversees the fallen warriors in Valhalla.

Frigg

Frigg was Odin's wife. She was a clever and attentive goddess by nature, she was the embodiment of regality. Everything that she did reflected her stature. She lived in the marshlands of Fensalir. Frigg was the mother of Baldur, Hod, and Hermod.

Loki

Odin once called Loki his blood brother. Loki is a half-giant and embodies the jötunn chaos within him in almost everything he does. One of the most catastrophic seeds of chaos that he sows is the children from his marriage with the Jötunn Angrboða. The three children, Hel, Jörmungandr, and Fenrir, all play a role in Ragnarök.

Thor

Considered a divine figure to the people of Midgard and hailed as a champion in Asgard, Thor, the god of thunder, was the son of Odin, husband to Sif, and a somewhat loving father to his three children. One of Thor's defining features was his hotheadedness when it came to the giants. He was always picking fights with them, and after he got his hands on his magical hammer, Mjolnir, the fights became a bit one-sided.

Baldur

Baldur was so beautiful that his mother made every living thing take a vow not to hurt him. Loki, being the personification of chaos that he was, decided to find out the one thing that had not taken the vow. Mistletoe. Yes. Mistletoe, of all things. He fashioned arrows out of mistletoe and managed to get Baldur killed, which eventually plunged the world into Fimbulwinter, the prelude to Ragnarök. Loki was soon after imprisoned for his crime.

Tyr

The Norse god of war, treaties, and justice, Tyr was known for binding Fenrir by sacrificing his hand to subdue the giant wolf. Tyr was the son of Odin and, as such, embodied his father's wisdom and valiance. The Romans equated Tyr to their god of war, Mars.

Var

The goddess Var was the goddess of promises, oaths, and agreements between two people. Her realm is concerned with more than just treaties, as she's concerned with punishing oath breakers.

Back in those days, oaths were taken upon items such as swords, rings, and shields. The people were expected to uphold their oaths, and if the said oath was broken, there was a terrible penalty for it.

Gefjun

Gefjun was the goddess of plenty, virginity, prosperity, and agriculture. She was responsible for keeping people's hearts full and for maintaining prosperity within storehouses. That's why her name originated from Gefa, which meant to give. She played a very integral role in agriculture, especially in the act of plowing.

Vor

Vor was a goddess of truth and prophecy. She was wise and ancient, having served as the handmaiden of Frigg ever since the end of the great war between the Æsir and the Vanir. Before that, she was an advisor to Odin.

Vor was originally from Jötunnheim, but after she pledged herself to Frigg, she made Asgard her second home and was known as an honorary Asgardian or Æsir goddess.

Syn

The goddess of refusal and rejection, Syn ensured to bar the way. She was also part of Frigg's entourage. She guarded the doors to Fensalir and would ask trespassers to leave. No one was allowed to loiter around Fensalir. Syn would also turn to violence if trespassers persisted.

Bragi

Bragi was the god of poetry and speech. After hearing about Bragi's skill, Odin assigned him to be Valhalla's bard. Bragi was more verbally inclined and musical as opposed to other gods in the Æsir pantheon. He had a wife, Iðunn, whose apples were the source of the gods' immortality.

In battles, Bragi took on the role of a war poet, inciting his troops to violence and slinging insulting poetry and mockery at the opponents.

Heimdall

The god of vigilance and foresight had the responsibility of being the divine sentry at the Bifrost to ensure that no unwanted being would walk through that bridge and cause any havoc. Heimdall was a fierce warrior, but just as he was fierce, he was also immaculately beautiful, with white skin and golden teeth. His hearing was so honed he could hear the grass blades grow.

Njord

Njord is a particularly strange addition to this group because originally, he was a Vanir, but after the Æsir-Vanir war, he, the patriarch of the Vanir tribe, was sent as part of the treaty to the Asgardians.

Njord was the patron god of the seas and had the most splendid fleet of all the Æsir.

Fulla

The deity of secrets, Fulla, was an asynjur in charge of maintaining Frigg's jewelry. She was also Frigg's confidante. She is said to hold domain over plentitude, but nowhere is her role as a goddess completely defined, putting scholars into a speculative position regarding her.

Hod

The god of darkness is blind and is unfortunate enough to be manipulated by Loki into killing Baldur. Baldur was Hod's brother. Hod was murdered by his half-brother Vali as vengeance for killing Baldur.

Eir

The patron of healing and medicine, Eir would come to your aid if you got injured in battle or even in a minor way. Those who were grievously injured on the battlefield looked to Eir to save them. She shares her name with a Valkyrie.

Vidar

Vidar, one of Odin's sons, is the god of revenge. Born out of Odin's union with the giant Gridr, he served as his father's avenger. The god is said to have been almost as strong as Thor. When given the chance, Vidar proved himself on the battlefield by showing his reckonable strength.

Saga

Some scholars suggest that Saga is just another of Frigg's alter-egos. She shared many characteristics with Frigg and often drank with Odin. She was a goddess known for her prophetic abilities and her wisdom.

Freya

Freya was also a Vanir originally, but after the war treaty, she was sent to Asgard and integrated into the Æsir tribe. She was quite beautiful and had a radiance to her personality, which made her perfect as the goddess of love, fertility, seiðr, and battle.

Freyr

Freya's brother was the god of peace, good weather, sunshine, fertility, and male virility. He was often connoted with a phallic symbol based on his male-sexual propensity.

Vali

Vali was the second god of vengeance, and it is said that he was conceived specifically to kill Hod.

Foresti

The child of Baldur and Nanna, Foresti was a god of justice and mediation. He was able to fix issues between two parties through his levelheadedness. He had his own courthouse where he was able to settle disputes. His axe was a symbol of negotiation.

Sfojn

Sfojn was an asynjur responsible for Freya's messages. She was also the guardian of engagements and betrothals. She was associated with love, caring, affection, and romance.

Lofin

Lofin was the sister of Sjofn and was associated with another facet of romance—forbidden love, unrequited love. She was the supporter of star-crossed lovers and would go on to bless their marriages. Lofin was so vehement in her pursuit of this mission that Odin and Frigg gave her permission to marry the forbidden lovers. Even though these marriages were considered banned, they were deemed valid.

Snotra

The elder sister of Lofin and Sjofn, Snotra was associated with wisdom, cleverness, and wit of all sorts, especially that connected to riddles and puzzles. She was the mother of a legendary sea-king Gautrek.

Hlin

The guardian of mourners, Hlin was also a member of Frigg's entourage and worked directly with the goddess by using Frigg's prophetic abilities to foresee if someone would get some bad luck. She would then intervene and help the people preemptively.

Ullr

Ullr, son of Sif, was a handsome polymath god. His father is not known, and much of what Ullr was all about remains a subject of speculation and mystery. His followers used to call him the Glorious One.

Gna

Gna controlled the wind and speed. She was also part of Frigg's entourage. She rode on a horse that could tread water and fly in the sky. She used to deliver Frigg's messages and would often run errands for the goddess.

Sol

Sol was the personification of the sun, according to some myths. She was the sister of Mani, the personification of the moon.

Bil

Bil and Hjuki represented the different phases of the moon, and because of this, Mani had taken them as his attendants.

The Vanir Gods

If the Æsir were renowned as the gods of warfare, might, and battle-wits, the Vanir, belonging to the second pantheon of Norse mythology, were associated with magic, fertility, zeal and zest, and nature. The Vanir knew a brand of magic called seiðr which could shape the future as well as prophesize it. The Vanir became key players in Norse mythology through their interaction, conflict, and union with the Æsir. The most well-known gods from the Vanir are Njord, Freya, and Freyr.

But what, weren't those gods covered under the Æsir part? Well, yes, but they were originally from Vanaheim.

While the Vanir gods are fewer in number, their stature and their importance were undeniable in Norse society.

Kvasir

Kvasir was considered the god of wisdom, poetry, wit, diplomacy, eloquence, and inspiration. He was born after the gods of both tribes gathered for a treaty and spat in a cauldron to represent their unity. From this mixed spit, Kvasir came into existence.

He was always eager to share his knowledge with others, often traveling to strange lands to find people to divine his wisdom. He was considered almost as wise as Mimir and Odin. He loved to wander, which eventually got him in trouble, as he was found by two dwarven brothers who murdered him and used his blood to form the Mead of Poetry.

Odin then stole the Mead of Poetry from these dwarves and used it often for wisdom and inspiration.

Nerthus

Nerthus was the goddess of abundance, stability, and fertility and was correlated with Earth. She was the sister-wife to Njord and the mother of Freya and Freyr, according to some sources. She was widely worshipped by the early Germanic tribes because of her ties to fertility and nature.

Odr

Some state that Odr is Odin's persona or an aspect of Odin from his dark days. Others claim that Odr was a god of madness and frenzy and was nothing like Odin. Odr was rough, callous, reckless, and vagrant, often leaving his wife Freya alone, causing her to weep and go out in search of him. Odr was the father of Hnoss and Gersemi.

While Odin was considered wise, tactful, and very considerate in his actions, Odr was considered like a loose cannon.

Hnoss and Gersemi

The goddesses of wealth, beauty, treasures, worldly possessions, and desires were sisters. They were Freya's daughters and were said to be indistinguishable from each other. Their names became synonymous with that of treasure, with Norse people calling their treasure hnossir.

Nanna

Nanna was the goddess of fertility and matronliness. She was symbolic of motherhood. She is said to have died from a broken heart after her husband died. Some accounts say she was grief-stricken after her husband Baldur's death, and threw herself into the burning ship with Baldur's body, not wanting to live a life without her husband.

Gullveig

She was the goddess of metals and gold. One can even say that she's the personification of purified gold. She triggered the events of the Æsir and Vanir war. She was burned three times and was born three times after she visited the Æsir. Her poor treatment at their hands is another factor that prompted the war.

The Æsir-Vanir War

Put yourself in the shoes of the Æsir gods for a moment and imagine how they must have felt when they discovered that instead of worshipping them as much as they should, the humans had turned to the Vanir gods and were paying more attention to them. While this was not exactly what triggered the war, as the Æsir were not *this* petty, this was certainly one of the contributors to the rising hostility.

The Æsir knew by now that the Vanir were able to use magic to manipulate nature, see into the future, and grant human beings boons like fertility, harvest, and familial bliss. Even this did not deter the relationships as badly as what later happened.

The goddess Gullveig came to the Æsir, apparently bearing good news. She said that she would teach them magic, including seiðr, and that she would be available here for a few days as a goddess-for-hire.

Initially, the Æsir gods were quite taken with her and were mesmerized by the magic that she was showing them. However, they soon discovered that they were becoming lenient and were resorting to debauchery and lewd behavior as they pursued their selfish desires through Gullveig's magic. In other words, their values of honor, kin, loyalty, and structure were compromised to such an extent that they perceived Gullveig to be an enemy, a spy, or, worst, someone sent to sabotage the Æsir gods.

Once they learned that this goddess had come to them from Vanaheim, it became apparent that their initial suspicion was correct. In their anger, the Æsir gods murdered her by setting her ablaze. But Gullveig rose from her ashes. This further incited the gods, as they were wary of Vanir's magic, and now here, it was being thrown in their faces again. So they set fire to her again. Again, she rose from her ashes. When they burned her a third time, Gullveig somehow made her way back to her realm and told the Vanir gods of what had happened.

This was the kindling that ignited the hostility between the two tribes. The Æsir and Vanir started to hate each other and even became fearful of what the other might do. The more these hostilities grew, the more it seemed imminent that a war might take place.

The Æsir and the Vanir came face to face on the battlefield, a plane that would be used again later for the last battle of Ragnarök. Here, the Æsir leader Odin flung his spear at the Vanir troops. This was a standard Norse ritual. Warriors would fling their spears into the enemy lines to show that the battle had begun.

The Æsir fought mercilessly, using brute force and their awe-inspiring weaponry. Many times in the battle, their strength lent them the upper hand. However, the Vanir used subtler warfare tactics such as magic and deception.

Both tribes realized as they kept fighting that their opponents were not mortal men or chaotic giants; they were gods. They could not keep fighting each other for eternity. Neither could win nor could they lose.

During the war, the Æsir damaged many of the Vanir's lands. The Vanir replied in kind by destroying the protective wall of Asgard.

This fighting ended only when both sides came to a stalemate. They decided to follow the Norse custom of giving each other tributes at the end of the battle. The gods came to an agreement that they'd treat each other as equals and that both sides would swap hostages. They solidified this agreement by spitting in a cauldron. The spit formed Kvasir, often considered a god and often considered a man.

The Æsir gods gave Hoenir and Mimir to the Vanir as a symbol of their new union. These hostages were also given to ensure that the peace would be maintained rather than disrupted again. The Vanir gave their patron god Njord, and his two children, Freyr and Freya, to the Æsir. The three Vanir gods taught the Æsir how to perform seiðr, therefore becoming important gods within the Æsir pantheon as well.

Hoenir and Mimir had terrible luck. Hoenir was elected the leader of the Vanir, while Mimir gave him counsel. However, Mimir would purposefully make Hoenir speak his own thoughts so that the Vanir would see that they had elected a fool for their leader.

But rather than think that Hoenir was idiotic, the gods perceived Mimir to be dumb and that he was not as wise as the Æsir had claimed. They beheaded Mimir and sent him back to the Asgardians. Although this act was hostile enough to restart the war, Odin reanimated Mimir's head so that he'd counsel the Asgardians instead.

Thus, the peace was kept and maintained. Odin gradually took the position of the de facto leader of all the gods. However, worship was decided to be equally split between the gods.

This chapter was a bit exhaustive in terms of subject matter. We discussed both the Æsir and Vanir tribes, their gods and goddesses, and how continuous friction between both tribes led to a great war between them. Moving forth, we will take a detailed look at some of the most popular gods and goddesses and learn about their traits, history, attributes, and mythology.

NORSE PANTHEON FAMILY TREE ILLUSTRATION

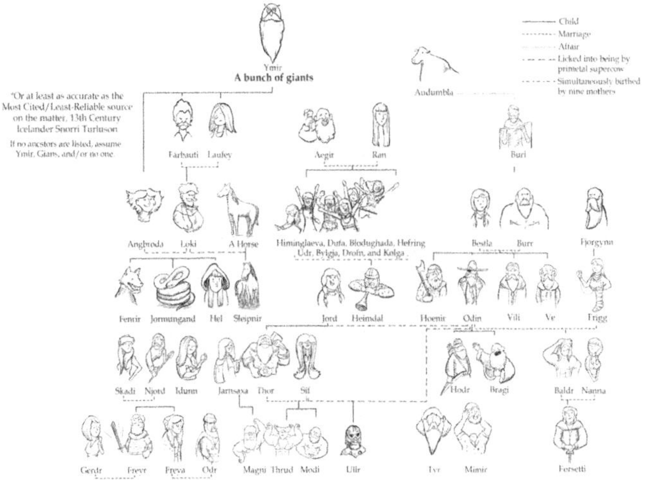

CHAPTER 4
THE A-LIST GODS OF NORSE MYTHOLOGY

Odin

His appearance has inspired the archetypal look of high fantasy wizards like Gandalf. Odin, with his piercing blue eyes, his white beard, and his magnificent spear that looks like a cane, appears every bit the wise, astute, powerful, and mystical god that he is. There is a good reason that Odin is at the top of the Norse hierarchy.

Norse mythology has shown us time and again that if you venture forth on a quest, you will eventually get what you desire and become all the more powerful because of it. This was also a belief rooted deep within the psyche of the Vikings. It was a necessity for them to have faith that their labors and toils will come to fruition because of the nature of their labors and toils. They had to sail across torrential seas to loot and plunder other lands, and quite often, they did not know where exactly they were headed or what kind of opponents they would face there. Or worst, if they'd find any loot there at all or not.

Odin represents the belief system of the Norse people, going on similar quests even though the outcome seemed bleak. One such example is when he sacrificed himself to himself and hung upon the Yggdrasil with his spear piercing him.

Odin was associated with the powers of battle, sorcery, shape-shifting, runic alphabets, healing, death, necromancy, royalty, wisdom, and warfare. He was a majestic god, but his majesty reflected the people who believed in him. There was a ruggedness to how he looked, but that ruggedness lent him character rather than making him look poor.

From atop his tower in his house, Odin can see throughout the Nine Realms.

He was the grandson of Buri and the son of Bestla and Borr.

His two brothers, Vili and Ve, helped him create the world from Ymir's body.

Odin was married to Frigg, with whom he had Baldur and Hod. Odin had other sons from other beings, including Thor. Sometimes, Odin gave in to the temptation of the beautiful giantesses in Jötunnheim. Thor was the result of one such union. Odin had yet another son named Vidar from a giantess called Grid. And another one called Vali from a giantess called Rind.

Like Loki, Odin could shapeshift and turn himself into an animal or a human. This was very vital to him, as it allowed him to wander about the realms without revealing his identity. Odin spoke in riddles and always uttered whatever he had to say in poetic phrases in a voice so soft that anyone who heard him felt that he was telling the truth, even when that was not the case.

Odin had innate control over magic, allowing him just to utter a single word and cause a torrent of fire to appear or to say another word and calm down the sea.

He was well-versed in battle but knew that he had to exercise control, what with him being the strongest and fiercest god out there. He could blind his enemies, imbue them with madness and fear, and render them fearful.

Odin could help his warriors become feral by making them go berserk. The Vikings often prayed to him and sacrificed to him before battles so that they, too, may go berserk.

Due to his wisdom and depth of knowledge, Odin could predict the fate of every human as well as see into their past. He knew about Ragnarök and how there was nothing that anyone could do to prevent it. Despite that, he took many precautionary measures to delay it.

Odin could make people ill just by thinking it and could even kill them with just a thought.

He was fond of his animals. He had two spiritual familiars, often considered an extension of himself, in the form of two ravens, Huginn and Muninn. He'd send them out every day so that they'd bring him news from all over the realms. They'd return in the evening and share what they'd seen by whispering in Odin's ear. Whenever they weren't exploring the worlds, they'd sit by Odin's side on his throne.

Besides the ravens, Odin had two wolves, Geri and Freki, whom he kept feeding from under the table whenever he dined. This was because Odin did not need to drink or eat to sustain himself. All he ever wanted was wine, and that, too, as a luxury, not a necessity.

Loki gifted Odin a magical steed with eight legs named Sleipnir.

Among his possessions was a powerful and magical spear made from Yggdrasil. Odin called this the Gungnir spear, and it had runes etched onto it.

He also had a ring Draupnir, which would sprout eight magical rings every ninth day.

Speaking of days, Wednesday is named after Odin.

Frigg

Frigg plays numerous major roles in Norse mythology. She was more than just Odin's wife and mother to Baldur and Hod. She was a goddess within her right, and at times, her matronly protectiveness made her a formidable opponent even for Odin.

While she was interpreted as a matronly goddess, she held sway over love, fertility, and marriage as well. But this was not entirely what made her stature so high up in the pantheon. The real reason was her gift for prophecy. She guarded this secret so well that she never told anyone what she knew of the future.

Odin knew this but never pestered her about it. He was well aware of her powers and had given her the honor of being the only other deity to sit on his throne. She resided in a marshland named Fensalir. Those who worshipped her often went out to marshlands to be spiritually close to her.

One of Frigg's prominent features was her entourage. She was always followed around by a court of women, of which a select few were her trusted confidantes and messengers. Her attendees included the asynjur of Asgard, who were also considered goddesses but lesser in stature than Frigg. Fulla, Lofn, Gna, and Hlin were some of the famous attendants of Frigg.

With her female attendees, Frigg populated Fensalir. This was considered a more feminine place within Asgard. A sanctuary, if you will.

Just as Odin went to extreme lengths to secure knowledge, Frigg went to equally extreme lengths to ensure the protection of her beautiful son, Baldur. When he was born, he was beloved by all because of his beauty. Frigg worried for him, especially when he started getting dreams in which his life was shown to be in peril.

Frigg went to every single thing in the known universe and asked them to take an oath not to hurt Baldur. Everything obliged, as everything loved Baldur too.

Such fortified was Baldur's protection that the gods often made sport of throwing things at him to watch them swerve in the air to avoid hitting him. Loki disguised himself and went to Frigg to find out how she had made this happen. In doing so, he found out that the only thing that Frigg hadn't gone to for an oath was mistletoe. Loki crafted an arrow from mistletoe and gave it to Baldur's brother, Hod. Hod was blind and was often left out of the throw-things-at-Baldur game because of his blindness.

The first time the blind brother participates in the game was when he shot the mistletoe arrow at Baldur and killed him.

Baldur's death was Frigg's first deep sorrow. Her second sorrow would come at Ragnarök, when her beloved husband, Odin, would die in battle.

Friday is named after Frigg.

Thor

His strength has earned him the title of almighty. Thor's strength and his dexterity over the elements, especially lightning, and thunder, came from his father, Odin, and his mother, the giantess Fjorgyn. His persona is as far apart from the Marvel comics and movies' version of Thor as far apart the authors of those comics in the '60s were from sobriety. Legend has it those authors were tripping on tabs upon tabs of acid and getting high on shrooms when they wrote those comics—and it shows.

The real Thor had red hair and a beard. He was associated with more than just thunder and lightning. He was a god of strength. Oak trees would bend to his command. He was not just an Æsir; he was the protector god of Midgard. While the modern version of Thor—as seen in the comics and movies—has quite the sense of humor and wit, the real Thor was not as smart or wise and was often an easy butt of the joke for many giants.

The giants loved making fun of him. They knew that Thor was ill-tempered and that it'd be very easy to get a rise out of him. Later on, when Thor got on more equal footing with the giants thanks to his magical hammer, Mjolnir, the teasing lessened, although it didn't completely cease. Thor would hit the giants over their heads with his hammer. He wasn't exactly defenseless against the giants. Whenever he was roused, he would make thunder and lightning appear in the sky. The loud grumbles of thunder and the wild flashes of lightning would scare the giants and send them back into their homes.

Thor lived in Asgard in a place called Thrudheim with his wife, Sif. His home had more than 500 rooms and was the known biggest house in Asgard. Thor and Sif had two children, Trud and Modi, and a stepson named Ullr. Thor had a son named Magni with a giantess named Jarnsaxa. The couple also had a servant named Thialfi and a servant-girl named Roskva.

He had two goats that used to pull his chariot. Whenever he would travel to far-off lands, he'd slay the goats and eat their meat. Upon his return, he'd reanimate them with

Mjolnir. Whenever Thor flew across the sky in his chariot, the sound from his wheels became thunder, and the sparks from his wheels became lightning, and both were seen and heard in Midgard.

Thor's magical hammer was one of Brokkr and Eitri's most powerful creations. It could tear down mountains, send out bolts of lightning, and hit any target from a distance. It would then return to Thor's hand on its own. The hammer had resurrecting powers as well. It could shrink and fit inside Thor's shirt if need be.

Thursday was named after Thor.

Baldur

Hailed as the god of light and purity, Baldur was the son of Odin and Frigg. He was extremely beautiful, often compared to the summer sun, and was said to be so pretty that his beauty made the flowers blush when they saw him. He was also quite fair, kind, wise, and gracious.

He had a home in Asgard named Breidablik, which was made of gilded silver. Only those who had a pure heart could enter his home. He also had quite an amazing ship, known as the Hringorni, which was also used as his funeral pyre after he was killed.

His death was a sad affair and was said to plummet the world into Fimbulwinter.

Vidar

Vidar had a terrifying title. The silent god of vengeance is what they called him. He was an Odinson, like Thor and Baldur. The title that he earned originated from the story in the Eddas that stated how he'd avenge his father's death. When Odin would die at the hands of Fenrir, Vidar would go and kill Fenrir. He'd also be one of the few gods who'd survive Ragnarök and would dwell in Idavoll. Vidar wore a thick shoe that he kept constantly mending. This shoe would help him plunge his foot down into Fenrir's mouth and reach down his throat to smash the wolf's heart. Norse shoemakers keep spare scraps of leather from the trimming of their shoes as a veneration of Vidar.

The reason he was known as the silent god of vengeance was rather morbid. Vengeance often forces a man to go silent, and in this silence, he plots his next steps and purifies himself of all other thoughts so he can focus on the vengeance at hand.

In some regards, Vidar was as strong as Thor. I would go so far as to speculate that his silence and his inclination to vengeance had somehow made him stronger, as Thor did not survive Ragnarök, but Vidar did.

Tyr

Tyr was the Norse god of war. He was not only a god of war; he was related to heroic glory, justice, and the formalities of warfare, such as treaties. Because of his enigmatic origins, he is considered to be one of the oldest deities in the Norse pantheon.

Of course, he was later on supplanted by Odin, whom many sources claim was the father of Tyr, while other sources claimed that Tyr was the son of a giant Hymir.

Tyr was depicted as being one-handed due to an act of courage. His limb was bitten off by Fenrir when the gods were trying to subdue the wolf. Because of Tyr's sacrifice, Fenrir was able to be bound until Ragnarök.

Had he not been one-handed, Tyr would have stood a chance against the hordes of Hel on Ragnarök. But due to his disadvantage, he was slain in battle by Garm, the guard dog of Hel.

Tuesday is named after Tyr.

Bragi

Bragi was so well-spoken and eloquent that he was given the title of Bard of Asgard. Because of his lyricism, he was also known as the skaldic god of poetry in Norse mythology.

Bragi was often found in Valhalla, singing to the einherjar and cheering them on with his tunes. But this was not the end of his domain. He would also use his poetry to boost the spirit of his warriors and use malignant verses to dishearten the enemies.

Fittingly enough, the god of eloquence had the youthful goddess of rejuvenation for his wife.

There was more to Bragi than just poetry. He was also the god of music, creativity, and artistic inspiration. He sported a long beard and had runes carved on his tongue.

Idun

Idun was the goddess of eternal youthfulness, or immortality if you will. She had great long hair and fair skin. She possessed golden apples that were the essence of immortality in Asgard. The gods would come to her and eat her fruit to maintain their youth and vigor. This made her a very central figure in Norse mythology, as without her, the gods would have been reduced to mortals.

Loki

Much can be said about the god of mischief with certainty except for one thing—was he truly a god? The Æsir saw him as one of their own even though he was only half Æsir and half Jötunnn. He was the son of Farbauti and Laufey. His mother was an asynja and his father was a giant.

It was very atypical that Loki was an Æsir from his mother's side because, in most circumstances, it was almost always the opposite, such as with Thor. This led Loki to adopt the name Laufeyson. It is speculated that Loki did this because his mother held more stature in Asgard than some giant and also because she was a goddess. Loki wanted everyone to acknowledge that he was the son of a goddess.

He embodied a lot of the chaos that the Jötnar were infamous for. He pursued mischief with such single-mindedness that he came to be synonymous with trickery.

Loki was married to a very loyal wife named Sigyn, who never left his side. From his wife, he had two children named Vali and Narfi. It was his other mistress, a giantess named Angrboða, with whom he had the spawns of chaos itself—Hel, Fenrir, Jörmungandr.

Some sources mistake Loki's penchant for trickery and mischief to be trademarks of evil. Loki wasn't exactly evil. He was not all good, but he wasn't strictly evil either. He was sociopathic, for sure, often resorting to mean feats of cunning to entertain himself at the expense of other gods and goddesses.

It was because of his cunning nature that he was seen as a frightening figure capable of being moody, sly, alluring, strange, and dangerous. He could shapeshift at will and was also well-versed in Seiðr.

Whatever his relationships with the Æsir were—and sometimes a lot of them were troubled—Loki revealed his true nature at Ragnarök when his children attacked Asgard. Loki stood by his children and even commanded their armies to defeat the gods and end the world.

One could say that the reason Loki resorted to such an extreme measure was probably because of how he was treated by the gods. After Baldur's death, Loki, for his many crimes, was chained with the entrails of his son Narfi and tied to three rocks inside a cave. A serpent was placed above him, dripping venom onto him. Only Sigyn remained by his side, sitting with a bowl to catch the venom. Whenever the bowl filled up, she'd go out to empty it. During that time, the venom would drop directly on Loki causing him unbearable pain, making him writhe in agony. Those movements would cause earthquakes. He'd stay chained until Ragnarök.

Perhaps it was this horrendous punishment that permanently pitched Loki against the gods, eventually causing their downfall.

Hel

Hel was the daughter of Loki and the giantess Angrboða. She came to be known as the queen of the realm of the dead after she was banished there. How she was banished, there is an interesting tale in itself. In Helheim, Hel tended to the souls of people who died from old age or illnesses.

Her appearance is described within her relation to Helheim. She is said to be half black and half white, the white half denoting her living self while the black or bluish part denoting her deadened self. Because of the circumstances that she went through and because of her inherent nature as Loki's daughter and the prophesized harbinger of Ragnarök, Hel was considered very cruel, harsh, cold, and threatening.

Odin threw her down into Helheim after he learned that she would be responsible for Ragnarök. Hel did not just resign to her fate. Rather, she crowned herself queen of the dead.

Her realm was surrounded by a large fence. The river Elivagar flowed next to the entrance. The gates of Hel were known as corpse gates. They were located in the Gnipa cave where Garm, the guard dog of Hel, guarded it and howled at the souls who entered.

Within Hel, Níðhöggr was trapped under one of Yggdrasil's roots and was always chewing at it. Whenever Níðhöggr heard the howling of Garm, he'd make his way to the entrance somehow and find the dead people and suck their blood, rendering them pale.

Those rendered pale by Níðhöggr's bloodsucking were then inducted into Hel's legion. Hel would use this army to challenge the gods on Ragnarök.

Within her hall, Hel had everything named after disasters. Her bed was called the sickbed. Her dining table was known as hunger. Her knives were called starvation. The curtains in the hall were called misfortune.

Heimdall

With skin as white as light and golden teeth that shone, Heimdall was a very radiant god. Besides those two attributes, he was tall, handsome, strong, and quite wise. He was tasked with guarding the Bifrost, the bridge that served as the sole entrance into Asgard. Heimdal was the son of Odin and, this is tricky to explain, nine mothers.

He was not very fond of sleeping. He slept less than a bird and was always honing his eyesight and his hearing. He could see as well as the most astute of hawks and could hear so well that he could listen to the sound of wool growing on the back of a sheep.

Heimdall had a place called the Himinbjörg next to the Bifrost. Whenever he was not busy protecting the Bifrost, he was riding around on his horse named Gulltopp. Gulltop was made entirely of gold.

Heimdall made it his habit to roam around humans and consult with them.

He would stand at the Bifrost with his sword, Hofund, by his side. He had an enchanted horn called Gjallarhorn. He'd use this horn at Ragnarök to signal the world's end. The sound of this horn was loud enough to be heard across all Nine Realms.

He would blow it thrice when he'd see the enemies arriving at the plane of Vigrid—the same plain where the Æsir-Vanir war had taken place. Upon hearing his horn, the gods would rush to the plains for that one last epic battle.

Njord

The Vanir god of wind, seafaring, hunting, fishing, and all maritime things, Njord was the chief of Vanir gods up until he was given as part of a treaty with the Asgardians. He was more than just a sea god.

Njord controlled fertility, peace, and wealth as well.

After moving to Asgard, he lived in a house by the sea. This was his favorite place in the entire realm, and he loved to spend his time there, listening to the sounds of the ocean and enjoying the sea wind.

He married a giant named Skadi, who fell in love with him after seeing his feet from underneath a curtain. But their marriage became very rocky after the two could not decide where to live. Skadi was a mountainous being, preferring the hills and mountains. Njord wanted to live by the sea. The two separated from one another soon after this dilemma could not be resolved.

They did have two children, Freya and Freyr.

Freyr

The Vanir, male god of fertility and prosperity was the son of Njord and the brother of Freya. He was associated with rain, harvest, and sunshine. Initially, he used to live in Alfheim as it was given to him as a toothing gift. His pristine nature reflected the nature of Alfheim and its residents, the elves.

The symbols of horses and phalluses were associated with him as he was associated with both. He had a trusty boar, Gullinbursti, and a ship, Skidbladnir, both of which he used to travel wherever he wanted to go. The ship was magical and could be folded into such a tiny size that it could fit inside a pouch.

Once, Freyr secretly ascended to Odin's throne to get a look at the Nine Realms. He saw a woman from there, a woman so beautiful that Freyr thought she was the prettiest thing he'd ever seen. He sent his servant Skirnir to woo the woman on his behalf. The servant was sent to bring the woman to Asgard.

Skirnir was given Freyr's magical sword to defend himself in the land of giants, where Gerd belonged. Gerd said that she wanted some of those magical apples that all the gods in Asgard were eating. When Skirnir said that wasn't possible, she refused the offer.

Skirnir then offered her other alternative gifts, even Odin's ring Draupnir, but Gerd kept refusing.

When Skirnir had exhausted all other options, he threatened her with runes, telling her that he'd curse her with the secret powers of the runes if she didn't come with him. Gerd agreed to marry Freyr because of this threat. She asked Freyr to wait nine days so that he'd yearn even more for her. The two got married, but at a serious cost.

Freyr didn't have his sword by his side anymore. It was given to Skirnir. In the battle of Ragnarök, Freyr would die without his sword in a fight with Surtr.

Freya

Freya was the female deity of sex, lust, eroticism, beauty, sorcery, gold, death, war, and fertility.

Freya knew magic, especially seiðr magic, which everyone coveted in the realms. She taught this magic to Odin and the rest of the Æsir too. Before this, this magic was only practiced by the Vanir. Freya had her own afterlife field for the souls of the bravely departed. This field was called Fólkvangr. It wasn't Odin but Freya who had the first pick of the souls who'd go to her realm. The rest would go to Valhalla.

Freya loved to travel. She had a chariot that was pulled by two cats. Sometimes she wore a cloak made of falcon feathers which allowed her to fly through the skies. Whenever she was not in the mood to fly or use her chariot, she rode her bore, Hildsvini.

Mimir

It was said that Mimir was so wise that his knowledge exceeded even Odin's. Mimir's name means rememberer, which is another indication of his knowledge and wisdom.

After the Æsir-Vanir war, he was beheaded by the Vanir, but Odin resurrected his head by embalming it with herbs and chanting magical songs on it.

Odin brought Mimir back to Asgard, where eventually, Mimir began guarding the Mimisbrunner well.

Odin walked with Mimir's head in his hands for hours and hours, asking him for counsel and advice. Mimir was more respected by Odin than any other god. Odin considered Mimir a friend and a confidante. A peer, almost. The two held intellectual talks that were ripe with knowledge and dripping with wisdom.

Even though they were such close friends, when Odin asked Mimir permission to drink from Mimir's well, Mimir said that he'd only let him drink in exchange for a sacrifice. Odin sacrificed his right eye by throwing it at the bottom of the well. Such was the price of Mimir's wisdom.

After taking a detailed look at some of the A-listers of the Norse pantheon, we're going to discover Norse Paganism and see how we can utilize our thus far theoretical and historical knowledge by putting it to practical use by integrating it in rituals, rites, and venerations of the gods and goddesses. This chapter concluded our theoretical learning of the gods, and goddesses, details about the Nine Realms, and Norse Cosmology. Moving forward, we will understand how runic magic works, how Norse magic in general works, and how we can practice that magic in our daily lives.

CHAPTER 5
NORSE PAGANISM

Characteristics of Norse Paganism

The Old Norse Religion was an organic religion, which is to say that it lacked a structured feel that was characteristic of Abrahamic religions. It didn't come into existence at once, complete with scriptures, commandments, and prayers. There were no central figures such as prophets or messengers to guide the people as a collective toward a religious goal. To that effect, Norse Paganism lacked confining dogmas, restrictive doctrines, and forced creeds. In this particular sense, the Old Norse Religion was rather liberating for its followers, so much so that the term religion does not really fit it all that well. It was more than a religion; it was a way of life and one that was not as high-maintenance or high-demand as Christianity.

Norse Paganism can be traced back to the Bronze and Iron Ages. By the 56th AD, the Roman historian Tacitus noted that the Germanic people whom he had observed followed a polytheistic religion. The religion underwent a gradual evolution, and it wasn't until the Viking Age that Norse Paganism propagated into the rest of the world and became known in a much deeper sense around the world. Norse people moved from Scandinavia and settled across Northern Europe, taking their religion with them.

But as grand as this propagation was, it was rather short-lived in the face of Christianity's missionary work. By the 8th and 12th centuries, Norse Paganism started to dwindle. Christianization took hundreds of years and eventually spread throughout Scandinavia as well, but one can never remove the roots of a culture from its people. Norse Paganism thrived in the form of folklore, stories, and poems among the Scandinavian people, preserving the faith in the long term. After almost a thousand years, although it had not disappeared completely, Norse Paganism came back in the form of neo-paganist movements such as Ásatrú, Vanatru, and Heathenry.

Norse Paganism had certain distinct qualities that set it apart from other religions of that time, especially the monotheistic, structured, and centralized religions such as Christianity. In contrast, Norse Paganism was:

- **Animistic**
- **Pluralistic**
- **Decentralized**
- **Polytheistic**
- **Immanent**
- **Orthopraxical**

Animistic

Followers of the Old Norse Religion believed deeply in the interconnected of things. Everything, whether it was a tree, a squirrel, or the water in a lake, was recognized to have agency. Nothing was more inherently important than anything else. Everything was considered to be equal and was believed to possess a spirit, knowledge, personality, and power. This was not because of some moralistic endeavor or for some holy purpose; Animism was believed to simply exist. Pagans perceived that everything played an important part in life as a participant in the grand interconnectedness of things. That's why they respected everything around them and tried to foster a spiritual relationship with things within the surrounding world.

This belief lent a very three-dimensional nature to every thing and action, taking away the binary "good" and "evil" or "virtue" and "sin" from it. The Norse worldview viewed things not as being either holy or profane but existing as equal. Divinity was considered an inherent part of the world as much as colors, sounds, and matter were. Desire, ambition, vanity, power, jealousy, and trickery were all considered natural feelings and driving forces.

But perhaps the biggest feature of animism was the belief that everything possessed a soul. One should note that the concept of the soul in Norse Paganism is very complex, where souls are multifaceted. Connecting with the spirit of things was a way of life for the Norse folk. They experienced Landvaetter (land spirits) within the land, Husevaetter (house spirits) in living spaces, the Jötunnn in the wilderness, and the Æsir as a manifestation of sacredness.

Animism allowed the Pagans to interact with the world around them in a way that felt most individually engaging to them, allowing them to add a ceremonial component in their everyday life, with each practice sometimes being unique to each individual, setting the premise that there was no one correct way to approach holiness and divinity, but countless. A cleric could attain divinity by worship, and a Viking could attain the same sense of sacredness through battle. A gardener could nurture his garden and send his love to the gods for blessing him with bounties, and an ironsmith could attain the same peace and purpose in making swords and axes. This equality in practice was all thanks to animism.

Rather than create a caste system in society, animism made a place for respect for all professions and endeavors amongst the people, truly allowing them to pursue what they passioned, making them excel in their endeavors, and truly allowing them to feel pride in their work.

Pluralistic

Building upon animism, we have pluralism, which is Norse Paganism's way of explaining how things are connected to each other. While Christianity takes a dualist approach, stating that everything falls into one of two categories (good and evil), and some Sufi sects in Islam follow a monist belief that all life comes from one source (God) and thus everything is in fact, a reflection of God, Norse Paganism entails that things are neither just good or bad nor do they come from just one source. Instead, Norse Paganism adheres to pluralism, which is the belief that all things contain multitudes within them.

Even the concept of soul, when explored through a pluralistic lens, reveals that Norse Paganism believes in a several-part soul. The gods and goddesses are looked upon in a similar fashion, where even the more traditionally malevolent deities such as Loki are not seen as just evil or bad but instead possessing a very complex character that contains a spectrum of traits, some of them good, others not so good, and some others just purely chaotic.

The concept of reward and punishment is a very dualist concept. Do this, that, and the other virtue, and you shall enter heaven. Become depraved in the way of sin, and you shall be spending an eternity in hell. Norse Paganism does not adhere to this belief, at least not in that strict a sense. Yes, those who die with honor in battle do go to Valhalla, and those who have spent a life of depravity and debauchery do indeed get punished in Helheim, but those are not the only two options; rather, they're two of many options of what happens to a person in the afterlife. For example, you can just die a regular death and go to Helheim, where all the departed souls dwell. In Paganism, Helheim is not seen as a place of punishment and torture. It is a realm, just like any other realm.

The pluralistic nature of Paganism gave its followers the freedom to pursue virtue of their own volition rather than be obliged to do virtuous things as a form of currency to gain entry into paradise.

This pluralism extended into their religious practices as well. Those who venerated Odin did so in a very different fashion than those who asked Freya for her bounties. Unlike Sufism or New Age religions, pluralism served as a deep foundation of the creation of the cosmos as well. Rather than just come into existence from one source, the Norse world came from the fire and frost of Muspelheim and Niffelheim, then Midgard came into existence from Ymir's body, and the dwarves and giants and elves similarly went on to inhabit their own realms, truly giving the creation story a pluralistic background.

Decentralized

Where did it come from? Who originated this religion? Was it a single source? No. Norse Paganism was decentralized from the very beginning. There's a very neat explanation for how it came to be.

The first part of the process is called decentralized tribal animism. In this part, small tribal communities start to venerate nature in their distinct ways. These veneration practices and beliefs are very localized to the decentralized tribes. Gradually, these tribes begin to exchange their customs with one another, often discovering in the process that their customs are very similar to each other.

In the second part of the process, decentralized tribal polytheism takes place, where after discussion with adjoining tribes and other people in the vicinity, the religion's nature-based animistic figures start to take shape. For example, Thor took on the role of the god of thunder, and Freya became known as the goddess of fertility. These deities were sometimes recognized in different communities through different names, resulting in the unification of the concept. But even then, the worship and veneration of these deities were very unstructured and folkloric.

Then, the development of decentralized cultus took place. Cultus refers to the parameters of religious practice. Once a civilization is advanced enough to form social classes and divide labor amongst them, the intellectual class thinks about religion and starts to formulate a cultus.

Afterward, the cultus is popularized as a central look of a polytheistic religion, therefore establishing a baseline praxis for that entire religion. In simpler terms, when you think of Norse Paganism and the first thing that comes to your mind are the Æsir and Vanir gods, Valhalla, Vikings, and so forth—that's the popularization of the centralized cultus.

Texts are then written about the cultus, especially if the dominant cultus is intended to propagate and popularize or preserve. Sometimes, these writings serve as scriptures for later followers of the religion.

Doctrines are then established, which lead to the development of transcendent-faith praxis, i.e., the answers to the big questions such as where we came from, where we will go after death, and other grand philosophical questions that revolve around transcendence. Eventually, these philosophies are molded into practices for the followers of the religion.

That being said, Norse Paganism remains just as decentralized today as it was decentralized almost a thousand years ago. It does not have any central scriptures. The

Eddas are historical texts that contain compilations of Icelandic folklore. They are not intended to be followed as scripture.

Polytheistic

Polytheism in Norse Paganism was a result of the decentralized, pluralistic, and animistic nature of the religion. The Norse Pantheon is populated with several gods and goddesses, many of whom we've discussed in detail. As Paganism was never centralized, different gods had different levels of popularity in different regions and times. Someone living by the sea might have venerated Njord more frequently than someone who lived in the mountains and venerated Ullr.

For someone coming from a monotheistic background, the concept might come off as rather jarring and even downright impossible, as many monotheists have provided the argument that if there were more than one god, there would be chaos.

While that's not entirely false—as seen in the numerous stories revolving around Loki—the truth is that having several gods in the Norse Pantheon provided followers of the Old Norse Religion with a rich backstory that had many complex deities instead of just one, allowing them to choose which god they'd like to worship based on the characteristics.

It also makes for interesting lore, where the gods, more or less on an even footing, have risen to challenges against them (such as Ymir and the frost giants) and have also challenged each other in battle, giving the followers a clear idea as to which god excels where and who is the strongest of them all.

One of the redemptive features of polytheism is it allowed the Norse Pagans to realize that the gods were fallible at times, and this created a relatability in the hearts of the followers, knowing that they were fashioned by the gods and thus was also prone to fallibility.

Norse Pagans had a very diverse array of venerating practices, including deity veneration, ancestor veneration, and spirit veneration.

Immanent

Speaking in a religious context, immanence is the opposite of transcendence. Sometimes, religions can be a little bit of both, but in most cases, you will see that religions are either immanent or transcendent.

But what does this mean?

Transcendent religions focus quite literally on transcendence. Abrahamic religions focus on transcending above this realm and into a better hereafter. Being a follower of a transcendent faith gives its followers a "higher purpose" that allows them to attain their desired afterlife by following a set of rules, practices, and worship. The primary goal of transcendent faiths is to elevate one's soul through meditation, enlightenment, devotion, and attaining knowledge.

In Christianity, for example, your actions either bring you closer to God or drive you further away from God. The nobler actions are known as virtues, and the profane ones are called sins. What constitutes sin and what constitutes virtue are detailed in the Bible. Christians adhere to the doctrines and dogmas written in the Bible to attain transcendence.

On the other hand, immanent faiths focus on the quality, fulfillment, actualization, and realization of your current life and the bond that you have with the people, creatures, and the world around you. The practices that encompass immanence are all about your immediate reality, your lived experience, and your well-being.

The goal of the faith here is to improve your present life by providing you with the structure necessary to cultivate harmony with the people and the environment around you. Rather than spend your life doing certain things in a certain way to ensure some rewarding afterlife, immanence requires you to improve your everyday life and to experience the joys of your faith in the things that you do.

It is the prevalent belief in Norse Paganism that you'll automatically join your ancestors in the afterlife (Hel) unless you devote yourself to dying in battle, in which case, you'll get to join the gods in Valhalla. This freedom allows the followers to pursue their goals and ambitions in life without worrying about what kind of afterlife they'll get.

Orthopraxical

The two main schools of religious thought are orthodoxy and orthopraxy. Orthodoxy concerns itself with the right beliefs, while orthopraxy is all about the right actions. Religions often have one of the two beliefs, but in some instances, they may employ both schools of thought. Take Islam and Hinduism, for example. They both employ both practices, where beliefs and faith in the doctrines fulfill the requirement for orthodoxy while actions such as fasting, prayer, pilgrimage, and keeping a karmic balance check the orthopraxy box.

Norse Paganism is an orthopraxical religion. It emphasizes experience, the integrity of practice, the continuation of one's lineage, and sustaining one's legacy rather than prioritizing faith and adherence to certain doctrines.

Orthopraxy provides a very individualized sense of what's right and wrong, meaning that what's right for one individual might not be right for the other. There's no centralized authority to dictate what's entirely right and wrong.

This doesn't mean that Norse Paganism does not have customs. There are customs and traditions carried out by descendants belonging to a certain lineage, but that is because of the orthopraxical nature of the religion rather than the orthodox nature, as maintaining one's legacy is an orthopraxical act.

Norse Beliefs

There are several distinct features of Norse beliefs that will provide you with a deeper understanding of how the Norse Pagans lived their lives and how they interacted with each other. Concepts like morality, hospitality, gifting, and harmony were integral to the functioning of Norse society.

. . .

Morality

In Norse Paganism, morality was not seen as some divine mandate by the gods. It was created very democratically by the people for the people. These moral concepts were concerned with the well-being of one's family, relatives, members of society, and living things in general. When the focus was on the well-being of people as opposed to the glorification of deities alone, traits like loyalty, modesty, self-reliance, hospitality, compassion, courage, wisdom, and kindness were emphasized. It was highlighted in the Hávamál that wealth was considered to be the most fickle of friends while wisdom was said to be the highest of currency, and as opposed to the temporariness of wealth, wisdom was eternal.

Frith

Frith is the experience that you feel when you get a sense of honest welcome from social interactions. Things like compliments, warm greetings, friendliness, drinking together heartily, and camaraderie contribute to the feeling of frith.

Simply put, it was considered to be the most basic love language to exist between people. When you extended someone frith, they felt close to you, and their loyalty was invoked as a result of your hospitable behavior.

Similarly, Norse hospitality was the primary mode through which frith was promoted in their society. When you demonstrated hospitality toward someone, it was a way of showing them respect, love, devotion, and goodwill—all of which were considered to be very important aspects in fostering relationships, whether familial, business-related, or romantic.

Gifting Cycle

The Norse folk were big on gift-giving, believing firmly in the process of reciprocation. They believed that a gift, rather than creating monetary obligation, was a sincere sentiment meant for the well-being of the individual being gifted with something. You could gift someone an item, a favor, your protection, love, your time and energy, space, and even sharing your belongings with them.

The gifting cycle was all about creating outcomes that brought about well-being by fostering harmony between two people. This created a sense of peace, purpose, and happiness throughout the community. The gift-giving cycle was related to wyrd and orlog.

Wyrd and Orlog

Wyrd means destiny. More than that, it represents the living world around you. It is the reality that you live in, the reality that is affected by your actions and their outcomes.

Orlog is the relationship between an action and its outcome. The outcome of your past actions dictates how your present reality is, and the present reality lays the foundations for the outcomes of your future.

Together, wyrd and orlog form the fabric of fate, serving as threads that weave in and out, shaping fates.

Inner-Yard and Outer-Yard

The Norse people had a very distinct boundary between their interior and exterior spaces. The interior spaces referred to their homes, their wall-bound communities, and their villages. Outside, the outer yard was the wilderness with all its mountains, forests, oceans, and wastelands.

Soul

The soul was considered a multi-part entity, with each part being equally important. The four main parts of the soul were hamr, hugr, fylgja, and hamingja.

The hamr was considered your outer appearances, such as your physical form, your personality, and your traits.

The hugr was your mind, will, emotions, and thoughts. Upon one's death, their hugr departed the body.

The fylgja was the essence of a person and could perform astral travel. It could take a certain shape, such as in the case of Odin, whose ravens Hugin and Muninn were his fylgja.

Lastly, **the hamingja** was the potentiality of a person, including their proclivities, inclinations, aspirations, strengths, and weaknesses.

. . .

Norse Rituals

The Norse Pagans were a celebrative people, finding festivity in each occasion. This was because the world they lived in was very adverse, and harsh, and took a heavy toll on them. The weather was ice-cold in the winter months, severely debilitating their ability to grow crops. Rival tribes would attack each other, claiming the lives of the townsfolk. Wild animals roamed about, posing a constant threat to the people. But despite all these hardships, the people found purpose and joy in their victories, both little and great.

Blót

Blót was a sacrifice practiced to get the goodwill of the gods and goddesses. The rituals were often carried out in large groups by the jarl or local chief. These sacrifices were both a time for people to venerate the gods and for the local chiefs to show off their wealth and prosperity.

Blóts happened four times a year—close to the winter solstice, at the spring equinox, at the summer solstice, and at the autumn equinox. If the people were having bad harvest or other troubles, they'd have additional blóts too.

Sumbel

This was a drinking ritual comprised of toasting, oath-taking, hails, reciting poetry, singing songs, and chanting. Sumbel had rounds during which the horn was passed in a circle, and each person hailed or toasted, then drank and passed the horn along.

The purpose of the sumbel was to invoke powers through words spoken in that holy rite. Oath-taking was a very common aspect of the sumbel, and given the nature of the rite, it was considered especially more meaningful and binding.

A sumbel started with an introduction by whoever was hosting the event. The first round then followed, during which all the gods and goddesses were hailed. In the second round, the ancestors and the great heroes were hailed. In the third round, people made oaths, spoke in a venerating manner, recited poetry, sang songs, and declared things.

As long as it was done in the proper vein, a sumbel could have more than three rounds. It ended with pouring out the remaining drink in the horn, then declaring that the rite is finally over.

Yule

The period between the winter solstice and the blót associated with it was given the title of Yule. It was a celebratory event marked by drinking alcohol, feasting for three days and nights, playing games, and singing. The Yule log was made from a large piece of oak decorated with yew, fir, and holly, and then runes were carved into it. This was to ask the gods for their protection. A piece of the log was preserved by the people to protect their families and to start the first fire of the new year.

Evergreen trees were decorated with clothes, food, runes, carvings, and decorations to invite the tree spirits to return in spring. People dressed up as goats to represent the goats that pulled Thor's wagon across the sky. They'd then go from house to house and perform plays and sing in exchange for food and drink.

Burial

The Norse folk were sent to the afterlife either by cremation or burial. Cremation was quite common among the earliest Vikings, who strongly held to the belief that smoke from the fire would help carry the deceased's spirit to the afterlife. The remains from the cremation were usually buried in an urn.

The burial locations for the dead were quite varied, with some graves being shallow (used for children and women) and others being burial mounds that could hold many bodies in the form of a grave field.

Boats were a symbol of safe passage into the afterlife. That's why boats had such a central role in funeral rites. Even some of the burial mounds were shaped in the form of boats. Vikings and Norsemen who were held in high regard were sometimes buried with their actual boats. Funeral boats were also used to send out the deceased into the sea, after which a flaming arrow was shot to set the boat on fire.

Some rituals were more prevalent than others when it came to burying the dead. The body was draped in fine clothes that were prepared specifically for the funeral. A celebration was held, cherishing the lived life of the deceased in the form of singing songs, drinking alcohol, eating food, and offering tributes. These tributes were known as grave goods and were almost equal to the value of the deceased's status in life. Someone who was a warrior was buried with their swords, axes, and shields.

Wedding

Before the wedding, the bride would remove a gilt circlet from her hair, representing the loss of her virginity. She'd then wear a crown at her wedding. The groom would have to acquire a sword from his ancestor's graves. The groom would carry his sword as a symbol of Thor's hammer. The bride and groom didn't wear particularly special clothes.

The weddings would take place on a Friday as it was Frigg's day, who was the goddess of fertility. The ceremony started by venerating the gods and getting their attention by sacrificing an animal for them. The groom would then give the sword that he'd gotten from his ancestor's grave to the bride so that she'd keep it for their future son. The bride would give her groom a sword, connoting that the job of protecting her was transferred from her father to her husband. Then the two would exchange rings and vows.

What followed was a feast in the hall, where the groom would first help his bride over the threshold by lifting her and then plunge his sword into a pillar. The deeper the sword went, the more luck and prosperity they'd have.

The couple was encouraged to partake in celebratory mead that they'd have to drink for the next month, which is where the concept of honeymoon comes from.

At the end of the feast, the couple would retire to the bed and consummate their love. The next morning, the wife's hair would be tied and covered with a cloth to show that she'd been elevated in her status as a wife. The groom would then provide her with the keys to the house, further cementing that status.

Birth and naming

After a baby was born, it had to undergo a certain ritual before it could be considered a real human being. Before the baby was named, they were not perceived as a real human being. One probable reason for this was so that people could emotionally protect themselves in case of the infant's death, as the mortality rate in infants was extremely high back then.

Once the baby was born, he was placed on the ground. The father came and picked him up and placed him inside his coat. This was done to symbolize that the father had accepted the baby as his. Once the baby was accepted, the father would inspect the child and see if the baby had any physical defects. If the baby were healthy, the father would sprinkle water over the baby. After that, the father would name the child and give him a gift. Gifts included things like rings, weapons, farms, and land deeds. Once this happened, the child was considered a real human being.

. . .

Seiðr

Seiðr was a magic practiced by both the gods and the humans. It was said that this sort of magic was related to influencing fate and interpreting one's destiny. There were wandering wise men and women who would use seiðr to both help and harm others. Its use was considered a bit of a taboo among some people, while others revered it as being a power so holy that Odin and Freya used it. Seiðr was used for clairvoyance and divination. It was a vessel for seeking out hidden things and for uncovering mysteries, both physical and mental. Seiðr could be used to heal the sick, bring about good fortune, and control the weather.

But just as it could be used for good, it could also be used for the opposite. It could be used to curse an individual, make a land barren by blighting it, and induce illness. Someone who practiced seiðr could intentionally tell false futures and send the recipients on a road to chaos and disaster.

Seiðr could even be used to kill people.

Its ambiguous nature was one of the reasons why it was seen as taboo by some.

Runes

Runes were used in the Old Norse Religion to make one's magical incantations permanent. They were carved into things such as wood, bone, stone, and metal so that their effects would last long.

According to the Eddas and the sagas, the runes held magical powers that could assist someone in predicting the future, protection from disasters and misfortune, and imbue things with a magical quality. Additionally, runes were used to write down spells, conjurations, and curses. In the next chapter, we will take a deep dive into runes and find out how they originated, how they worked, and how you can use them in your life.

This was certainly a very packed chapter, containing vital information about the characteristics of Norse Paganism, the beliefs held by the Norse people, and the rites and rituals that they observed. Going forward, we will take some of those rituals and study them in a detailed manner to get some practical understanding of how to be a practicing pagan and how to incorporate those rites in our everyday life, starting with runes.

CHAPTER 6
THE RUNES

A Brief History of Runes

The Germanic-speaking people used the runic alphabet for reading and writing from as far back as 150 AD. The Elder Futhark script came into prominence around 700 AD, and the Younger Futhark script, which was a hallmark of the Viking Age, came into prominence around 790—110 AD. Other forms of the script also evolved, including the Anglo-Saxon Futhorc writing system. England had been using runes from the 5th century until the 11th century. Scandinavia, on the other hand, kept using the runes well into the Middle Ages and beyond.

Many runestones were erected throughout Scandinavia, which today serve as a strong connection with the history of the Germanic-speaking people.

Runes were comprised of vertical lines that had branches/twigs jutting out diagonally, upwards, downwards, and in a curved fashion, depending on which rune was being written. They could be written from both right to left and left to right. Each rune represented a phoneme, which was a speech sound, and had a name comprising of a noun that had the same starting sound as the associated rune.

The origins of the runic script date back to 160 AD on the Vimose comb from Denmark. The inscriptions on that rune were so confident, mature, and prolifically used that researchers deduced that such an advanced form of usage must come after hundreds of years of experience in writing in runes. While that gives us a timeline of how old the runes were, how exactly did they come into being?

Archaeological evidence has directed towards Greek and Roman alphabets, considering that unstandardized Greek might have reached the Germanic speakers by way of travelers serving as middlemen.

While those origins are fitting for academic and archaeological purposes, those of the faith believe that Odin gained the knowledge of the runes after sacrificing himself to himself and hanging from Yggdrasil for nine days and nights without food or drink. For the devout, this explanation is far more credible, romantic, and grandiose than, say, stating that the script came into being as a result of Greek and Roman languages.

By 500 AD, the runic script had fanned out across Sweden, Denmark, and Norway, and had spread to outposts in England, Germany, Poland, Russia, and Hungary. Because of this expansion and how different people used them, four main scripts came into being:

- The Elder Futhark
- Younger Futhark
- Anglo-Saxon Futhorc

- Medieval Futhark

There were great variations among the scripts, leading scholars to the conclusion that the Futhark scripts were not used as a definitive script for one language but instead for many different Germanic languages spoken across a vast area. The shapes of these runes differed, as well as their layout, order, medium, and usage depending on the regional, chronological, and social differences. That's why there was never actually a standardized runic alphabet.

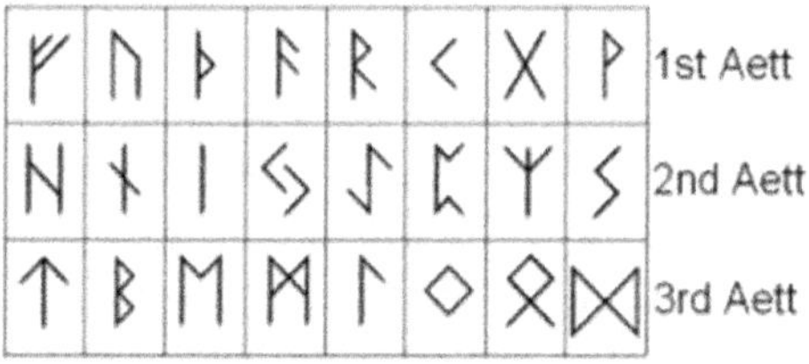

The Elder Futhark

Elder Futhark

This was the earliest classified runic script and was widely used in the Germanic world until 700 AD. 24 characters formed the elder Futhark script, with the first six of the alphabets forming its name 'Futhark'. The runes are grouped into three rows of eight, and each group is called an aett. Each rune was named after things that started with that sound.

While there are examples of written manuscripts in the Younger and Anglo-Saxon Futhark, there aren't any examples when it comes to the Elder Futhark, even though it was used to write Proto-Germanic, Proto-Norse, Proto-English, and Proto-High German. What survives today of the Elder Futhark is barely 400 inscriptions, and even those have shown quite a lot of wear and tear. As of now, they're partly legible. The real number of the inscriptions is unknown, presumed to be lost to time and space. What remains of the Elder Futhark today has been recreated using Younger Futhark and the Gothic and Anglo-Saxon variants.

Some of the inscriptions found were on wood and metal. Other surfaces that had Elder Futhark inscriptions included coins, military equipment, jewelry, combs, brooches, and runestones.

Younger Futhark

After 700 AD, the Elder Futhark was merged and adapted into the Younger Futhark script, mostly reserved for writing Old Norse—the language of the Viking Age. The original 24 characters were replaced and reduced to 16 runes. The 10th century saw the Younger Futhark being widely used all over Scandinavia.

The earlier of the Younger Futhark inscriptions were discovered in Denmark, leading them to being called Danish runes. Another variant came into light in the form of Norwegian-Swedish runes. Yet another variant became prominent, this one being quite minimalistic because it was staveless.

More than 3000 runic inscriptions in the Younger Futhark were discovered from the Viking Age, many telling stories about ownership, inheritance, politics, raiding, religion, magic, travel, literature, and myth.

A lot of the runes were found to be commemorating and celebrating the dead in the form of prayers, obituaries, signatures, and statements saying that the deceased was a good warrior, a noble man, a striving farmer, and so on.

Some of the Younger Futhark runes have signs from the carver on them, signifying that carving runes must have been considered a very specific skill at that time. As Seiðr was considered a very female-oriented task, runes were considered a male-oriented skill.

Anglo-Saxon runes

(5th to 11th centuries)

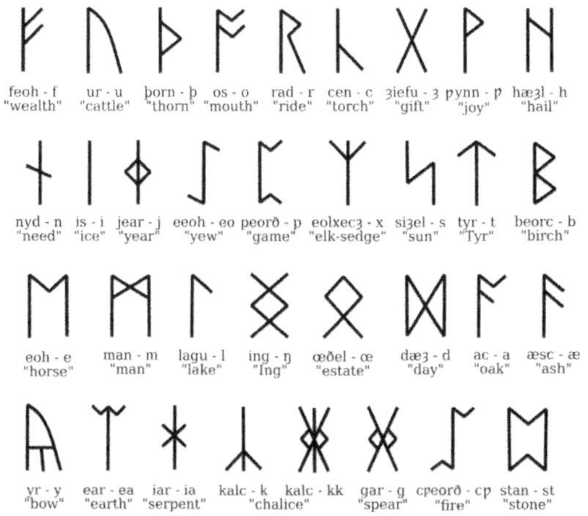

Anglo-Saxon Futhorc

The Anglo-Saxon Futhorc began somewhere around the 5th century in Britain and Frisia. Unlike the Younger Futhark, the Anglo-Saxon Futhorc added runes to the script so that they'd be able to use them in writing old English and old Frisian. Some of the inscriptions that have survived include stone crosses, coins, weapons, and personal items. But the number of these inscriptions is even less than those of the Elder Futhark at just under 200.

Between the 7th and 9th centuries, more of these runes were seen on coins, hinting that the usage went beyond just commemorative; these were practical runes used to denote the value of coins. As Christianity came into the scene in the 7th century, it left its mark on the Anglo-Saxon Futhorc, reforming some of it and competing with it in inscriptions until a time came when Latin was being used side by side with the Futhorc. The Anglo-Saxon runes held their own until the 10th century, after which they were replaced entirely, and their usage came to an abrupt halt.

Medieval Futhark

The Younger Futhark shaped medieval Futhark. Between the 10th and 11th centuries in Scandinavia, this script evolved from the Younger Futhark and was used quite consistently throughout the 13th century. It had the 16 Younger Futhark runes but with some tiny modifications to set them apart from the Younger Futhark.

The Symbols, Meanings, and Usage of Runes

Pop culture, especially video games and high-fantasy franchises, have created this picture of runes as being latently magical and downright mysterious. From *The Elder Scrolls* to games like *Kingdoms of Amalur,* runes have become a staple of Norse-inspired video games and Western RPGs, providing gamers with an extra layer of immersion in the form of this mythical language that is so quintessential of Tolkien-esque concepts of magic and fantasy.

But before they were a fantasy trope, runes were being used by the Germanic and Nordic people a thousand years ago for writing, magic, and divination.

As for what they are, well, the word 'rune' means 'mystery.' Oracles used in the past to help others gain insights into situations or answer questions. In modern paganism, runes have been used to guide you through any issues, help you tackle problems, and show you what can likely happen in the future. They must not be confused with fortune-telling, as runes are riddled with mysticism, and quite rarely do they ever give a straight answer.

Runes offer variables, hints, and suggestions on how to act if a certain probability happens in the future. When you use runic magic or runes for divination, you'll discover that there's a lot of room for interpretation and intuition.

But why? Why is that so? Well, think of it from a logical point of view. The future is not fixed. Thousands, if not millions, of variables affect the future, with the tiniest change in one variable resulting in an entirely different outcome. If the future isn't fixed, then there's no fixed way to tell what exactly is going to happen. But runes can help you cast light on that uncharted territory and allow you to follow the path of the optimum outcome, provided you use their guidance well.

With the guidance of the runes, not only can you anticipate likely possibilities in the future, but also use that knowledge to your advantage and change the outcome.

While there is innate magic in the runes, the general principle that modern paganism follows when working with runes is that when you cast runes, your conscious and subconscious align, allowing you to communicate with the message of the cast runes. It is inferred that the runes that are cast are not random at all but are chosen by your subconscious. That is to say, this is not a definitive explanation for how runes work but one interpretation of modern pagans. Other pagans state that the gods and the Norns themselves decide the order of the cast runes in order to help you. Others state that the runes possess power of their own and have the ability to channelize their magic in runic magic, casting, and divination.

That's why it is so fitting that they are named runes because it remains a mystery as to how they truly work. What matters is that they work, they are potent with magic, and they are one of our best methods to contact the ethereal, the powerful, the fate-weaving, and the holy.

The meanings of the runes are tied to universal forces that change and evolve with time. These forces, elemental in nature, are just as relevant today as they were thousands of years ago. But since these forces have a sentient nature, their manipulation of the runes makes rune reading a very subjective and personal matter.

I would say that rune reading takes a lot of practice. Like any art, the more you hone it, the better you'll get at it. Since it's a religious act and a very magically charged one at that, you must always approach this craft with the respect and honor it deserves. While books, guides, online tutorials, and DIYs can help you practice runes, you should first form a bond with them by studying their meaning, understanding the power they hold, and learning about how they were used in the past and how you can use them in a respectful manner. When using runes, you must always trust your intuition, as divination and oracle reading are very intuition-heavy activities.

Each rune has an associated deity, animal, or entity with whom it is connected. Fehu, for instance, represents cattle.

Thurisaz is associated with the giants. Uruz is a symbol of strength.

While some of the meanings of the runes are decipherable, the greater mystery is still shrouded in mysticism and is very subjective. That's because runes and their meanings evolve and change with time. Everyone interprets them in their own way, with relative meanings. However, the primary aspects of runes that are common throughout include three main characteristics:

- The symbol of the rune and what it represents
- The name and the meaning, along with the sound and the letter value
- The energy, deity, trait, and spirit embodied by the rune

The Elder Futhark—which are the runes that we'll be studying—are sorted into three sets of eight runes known as the aettir. These aettir are respectively known as Freyr's Aett, Heimdall's Aett, and Tyr's Aett. Symbolically, the three aetts represent the three parts of life's cycle. The first set of runes represents finding one's footing in the material world through the accumulation of wealth and an elevation of status. Things like cattle, communication, negotiation, vigor, strength, and business wit are related to the first set. The second set is all about increasing one's growth, maturity, and wisdom. This set holds runes like fate, harvest, abundance, and obstacles one must overcome. The third set of runes is related to developing one's legacy and spirituality. These runes contain birth, intuition, inheritance, and community.

While, yes, some of the meaning of the runes is lost as they once belonged to the Old Norse people and haven't exactly been transcribed into a place, one should not lose hope about this lost legacy as runes have a way of revealing their meaning to the seekers, the searchers, and those who are patient enough to let the runes communicate with them.

Without further ado, let's take a look at the runes and their meaning.

Fehu

Phonetic Value: F

Pronunciation: "FAY-hoo" "FEY-who"

The literal meaning of Fehu is wealth, power, and cattle.

Fehu is symbolic of two branches growing off a tree. It can also be seen as the two horns of a cow. While the literal meaning connotes cattle, cattle itself was a signifier of a family's wealth and power in the past. You could pay off your debts with cattle. If a man was killed unjustly, the blood price would also have to be paid in cattle. If someone did not own their own cattle, the tribe's or clan's cattle were considered to be theirs, provided that they were a person of status. A bard was said to have a blood price equal to that of a king because he was a learned man and a reservoir of tales, beliefs, and anecdotes.

In that sense, cattle were considered a means of exchange, much like we use money today.

If you want to interpret Fehu, know that its appearance signifies the arrival of success and wealth. If the cast shows Fehu, it is considered fated that your hard work will be rewarded soon. While the concept of wealth is ever-changing, given that once cattle were used as currency and nowadays we have so many types of currencies ranging from gold and silver to bitcoin and NFTs, Fehu always signifies an improvement in your business affairs and an increase in your earnings. However, there is a caution attached to the appearance of Fehu. This money does not come scot-free. It has to be applied to things that have some solidity and permanence, for example, real estate or resources whose value will appreciate over time. Fehu also highlights the boost in self-esteem that comes with the attainment of wealth. It is a metric of how one can pursue their dreams and goals with the wealth that they have received. If you see Fehu, it means that your dreams are going to be realized soon through the catalyst of money.

The inverted or reversed meaning of Fehu suggests the loss of wealth or the disadvantages that come with hoarded wealth. Money can corrupt people, sever bonds between friends, cause tension between two parties, and may even destroy one's reputation if said money is spent recklessly. A reversed Fehu can serve as both a warning and foreboding that your wealth might be in danger if you choose to use it in a vile manner. An inverted Fehu can be a warning from the gods to be wary of all the negative aspects that come with wealth. If you were about to embark on a new business venture, an inverted Fehu could be a warning sign, telling you that your venture might not end up the way you thought it would. If it shows up reversed, it could indicate you losing your personal possessions or coming across struggles that cause your self-esteem to dip.

Uruz

Phonetic Value: U

Pronunciation: "OO-rooz"

With its literal meaning being Aurochs, the powerful and extinct ox whose size was between a bison and a mammoth, Uruz is symbolic of power, endurance, wild potential, emotional strength, and vitality. The Vikings used to revere the horns of the Auroch, from which they drank. Another aspect of this rune is its relation to the god Ullr, who was the god of archery, winter, and hunting. In Germanic folklore, Ullr was known as the god of the hunt.

This rune connotes unhindered power. Raw, untamed, physical force. Additionally, this power can be sexual as well, especially when it comes to male sexuality. If this rune shows up for a man, it signifies a change in the man's masculine powers imminently. If it shows up for a woman, it can be a sign that a man will come into her life and affect her either romantically or in a physical (sexual) way.

It wouldn't be uncommon for this rune to show up for athletes, hunters, military personnel, and people who exert their physicality in their fields, such as bodybuilders, MMA fighters, parkour artists, and so on. If Uruz shows up for any of the aforementioned people, it can be a sign that their strength will be reinforced. It can also be a warning sign if they're overexerting themselves, telling them not to abuse their powers to avoid potential injuries.

If you've drawn Uruz, it is telling you that now is not the time for being subtle or passive. It's time to be active and take advantage of the opportunity available to you by being powerful.

An inverted Uruz could be a sign of emotional and physical weakness. Someone around you may be using your energy against you, such as by sapping it from you by making you doubt yourself, sabotaging your plans, or downright degrading you. If it shows up inverted, it's telling you that you have to look out for brutality and violence from others.

Thurisaz

Phonetic Value: Th

Pronunciation: "THUR-ee-sahz"

The literal meaning of this rune is thorn. Why thorn? Well, the frost giants had a son named Loki (you know Loki, big mischief monger, chiefest of calamities, father of Fenrir) who proved to be a thorn in the side of the gods time and again. Thurisaz also means giant, representing the giants and all the danger they represented. You can also look upon Thurisaz as being symbolic of Thor's hammer. It's a very interpretive rune, leaving quite a lot to one's intuitive powers and imagination.

However, this much is certain in its interpretation—the rune warns you to take precautionary measures, to defend yourself against potential thorns that might be lying in your path, and to overcome conflict with your intelligence. If you get this rune in your reading, you should protect yourself by taking the necessary measures. Thurisaz can indicate an ambush from an enemy.

In its representation of a thorn, Thurisaz comes bearing a gift: The wisdom that comes when you're pricked by a thorn for the first time. You will always remember the pain and will be wise enough to avoid thorns whenever you see them in your path again. It's a lesson, a painful one at that, but you have learned it and are now better suited to deal with similar situations in the future. These situations could be harsh outside forces, critical situations in your everyday life, health hazards, some treachery by a foe posing as a friend, or someone opposing you. You have to cultivate discipline and adapt to the change with the realization in mind that things that are fated to happen will happen, and it is only within your power to act bravely and honorably in the face of those things and to endure hardships so that you can get out on the other side.

An inverted Thurisaz means that you're being too obstinate in the face of change. Do not resist, and do not run away from adversity. Think of the long-term instead of just the immediate outcome. You must understand that these hardships are part of life, just as much as a thorn is part of a rose. Do not ignore these problems; otherwise, they will become too big to deal with later on.

Ansuz

Phonetic Value: A

Pronunciation: "AHN-sooz"

Now, this is an important rune, literally meaning god. It represents the breath of Odin. Belonging to the most powerful Norse god, Ansuz is related to wisdom, divinity, culture, creativity, communication, drawing, music, art, inner knowledge, and spiritual growth.

If Ansuz shows up in a draw, be on the lookout for a guiding figure, someone with knowledge and authority, such as a teacher, parent, or employer. This figure can guide you toward a positive life-changing event. You can potentially get a promotion, a raise, or a bonus in your line of work. If you're a creative person, you might be on the verge of your next big project, such as a book or a work of art. If you have been facing a problem for a long time, now might be the time that this problem gets resolved. You will get assistance from someone wise and knowledgeable. This can also hold true in religion. A priest or a spiritual leader may help you untangle some existential crises. Lastly, it can be a symbol of the divine trying to get in touch with you with a message of creation, growth, and guidance.

If this rune shows up inverted, understand that the authority figure who's about to come into your life is going to be a hindrance to your goals. Someone who might be posing as an authoritative figure might be trying to deceive you. Be extra wary of that. The hindrance could very well be within you. Perhaps you're resisting someone's help that you shouldn't resist. Perhaps someone is trying to help you out, but you're being too obstinate and prideful and aren't accepting their help. Whatever wisdom is out there in your immediate circle of contacts, you must accept it and invite it toward you.

Raidho

Phonetic Value: R

Pronunciation: "Rah-EED-ho"

Raidho means journey and riding through a chariot or a wagon. This rune is indicative of the life journey of a person. Raidho signifies that the journey is more important than the stops along the way. One's course in life is decided by the Norns. Raidho reminds us that great events in our life are beyond our control. These include birth, death, winning, losing, suffering, joy, hardships, ease, and everything in between. One must understand that fate is to be respected, not to be controlled. By flowing along fate, one can channel it and become one with it. There is nothing to gain by averting fate. Even the gods knew that. They knew that they weren't able to stop Ragnarök.

When Raidho shows up in a rune reading, it reveals that you're about to embark on a journey, the outcome of which will be in your favor and will result in positive changes in your life. This rune signifies a change in your career with new experiences and insights awaiting you in the future. Raidho wants you to let what's going to happen, happen. All attempts to try to stop the inevitable will result in failure. It can also mean a spiritual journey through which you will become a wiser person. Raidho has a celebratory nature, often revealing reunions with old friends and family members, telling you that if you're feeling lost and down and defeated, worry not, for emotional reinforcements are arriving soon in the form of familiar faces.

An inverted Raidho indicates that the journey you'll embark on will stray you from your primary path. If there's a career change or a business move, it might disrupt your personal relationship and will likely result in a negative outcome. If you had planned something, there will be a delay in those plans. Whatever you intend will be met with challenges and hurdles. However, these challenges, delays, and hurdles will lead you to newer opportunities rather than rob you of existing ones. When a reversed Raidho shows up for a spiritual reading, it indicates the need to push past the agitations, frustrations, and worldly delusions that are holding your spiritual journey back.

Kenaz / Kaunan

Phonetic Value: K

Pronunciation: "KEN-ahz"

Kenaz literally means torch. What that actually stands for is the flame of divine inspiration. With that fire comes creativity, inspiration, vitality, energy, and the banishment of darkness. This rune indicates a rebirth through sacrifice. Creativity through fire. Artists get this rune, especially when seeking a reading about their artistic ventures.

Like a torch, the message of Kenaz is that of a warm welcome. The cold dark has been dispelled. Come into the radiance. Come into the light. Seek shelter here. Rest, if you will. You are in a safe place.

Its interpretation concerns finding solutions to long-standing problems. If you've been struggling with hurdles for a long time, your solution is right around the corner. Kenaz represents that eureka moment that will lead you to discovery. Like flames, sometimes the guidance that Kenaz hints towards will be fiery and intense.

When it shows up reversed, it's a sign of the flame being darkened. A friendship might be ending, a journey may be coming to an end, or a source that you were using for inspiration all this time might be petering out. This must not stop you from achieving your goals. Instead, be patient and bide your time in the trough before you crest again.

Gebo

Phonetic Value: G

Pronunciation: "GHEB-o"

With its literal meaning being generosity through gifting, Gebo represents everything that has to do with the act of giving. It is one of the few runes that cannot be inverted.

It manifests that a gift will be given shortly. Even a marriage proposal or an opportunity to advance your business. Someone is going to come into your life, either romantically or materially, who will change it in a bountiful manner. Sexual union is also one of the meanings of Gebo. If it comes up in a paired reading with Uruz, it may indicate a fleeting encounter. A very intense encounter, at that. It can be cultivated into something more if needed.

Wunjo

Phonetic Value: W

Pronunciation: "WOON-yo"

Wunjo resembles the flag planted on a battlefield after a victory. A victory that results in song, joy, celebration, and rejoicing. That is what Wunjo means. This rune encompasses joy, pleasure, success, comfort, and harmony. It is a call to positive manifestation, stressing the need to take affirming action toward the achievement of a goal.

When Wunjo shows up in a reading, it is telling you to shed your ego and look to a higher purpose and meaning. Align yourself with the universe and become truly mindful of the present so that you can best equip yourself to achieve your goals. Wunjo represented the Law of Attraction before the Law of Attraction was cool. If Wunjo shows up in a reading, especially when you were trapped in a pessimistic and negative space, it is telling you to think positively and adjust your thinking attitude.

An inverted Wunjo says that your journey toward a goal is going to be difficult. It's going to take longer to reach your goal than you expected. However, you don't have to worry, as an inverted Wunjo is an invitation to strive harder rather than retreat. An inverted Wunjo is a sign that the difficulties in your life have severely altered your mentality and that you need to get in touch with your roots and push the reset button on your mindset.

Hagalaz

Phonetic Value: H

Pronunciation: "HA-ga-lahz"

Hagalaz means hailstone. It is the herald of the wrath of nature and the destruction brought about by uncontrollable force. At its core, the rune tells of necessary destruction, a destruction seen in Ragnarök. It was needed to bring about the rebirth of a new world.

This is one of the few runes that cannot be pulled inverted.

When Hagalaz appears, it is an indication that one should prepare for the future and ditch all thoughts of the past. Often, the past holds us back and has a psychological hold on us in the form of emotional blocks and trauma that can debilitate us. Where it represents destruction, Hagalaz also represents rebirth. Let the past go, is what the rune says, and embrace the emotional destruction that shatters you and then makes you anew again so that you can grow in the future.

It is a heavy concept but put it into a simpler analogy, and it will be easier to understand. Someone goes through a terrible breakup or gets fired from their coveted job, or a loved one passes away. All these things have happened to many of us at some point in our lives. While it is right to grieve and become sad at loss, it is pertinent that once that grief has been processed, one must move on, get over that ex, look for a new career opportunity, spend time with one's living relatives and cherish them, and so forth.

Nauthiz / Naudhiz

Phonetic Value: N

Pronunciation: "NOWD-heez"

Nauthiz symbolizes necessity. It is a rune about endurance, willpower, and the factors that sometimes demand endurance and willpower; trouble and constraint.

Imagine, if you will, a worker who has been necessary personnel at a factory for thirty years. He has learned all the tricks of the trade, knows his way around the machinery, and is extremely adept in his craft. One day, he arrives at the factory and sees that a robot has replaced the job that he has been doing for so many years. He is rendered obsolete. What does this man do in the face of such an unconquerable difficulty?

That is what Nauthiz is all about—a chance for someone who has fallen short to step back and take into account what needs to be done. It is a test of one's endurance and willpower. Does that factory worker simply succumb to his obsolete fate, or does he adapt and start his own small business, one that caters to the refinement of handcraft rather than the heartlessness of machine-made things? He relearns, he finds another way, he perseveres, and most importantly, he reevaluates.

That is the interpretation of Nauthiz as well. If faced with setbacks, turn to the route of introspection and growth.

While some claim that Nauthiz cannot be reversed as it is a symmetrical shape, others state that a reversed Nauthiz can indicate the need for even more restraint than before in the face of overindulgence. Rather than material, focus on the spiritual. Learn to let things go and take stock of what is truly needed and what is purely excessive. Understand the difference between the two.

Isa / Isaza /Isaz

Phonetic Value: I

Pronunciation: "EE-sa"

Isa means ice. A simple rune, Isa can be considered the opposite of Kenaz. Where Kenaz was fire, Isa represents the stillness and purity that is characteristic of ice. While the fire is kinetic and instills movement, ice is potential and requires stillness.

It is one of the runes that cannot be reversed.

If Isa shows up in a reading, it wants you to meditate and recharge before you take action. Now is your time to rest. Be still. Once the metaphorical ice thaws, your direction will become clear. Beneath the cold and still and lifeless layer of ice lies a world waiting to bloom. All it is waiting for is the right season. Thus, so too should you wait as well. Do not abandon your goals nor lose sight of the things that you have to achieve. Just take a brief break from them while you meditate and improve your inner self.

Jera

Phonetic Value: J (J in Germanic languages)/ Y (like the "y" in year)

Pronunciation: "YARE-a"

Yet another irreversible rune, Jera means harvest, a time of plenty, summer, completion, reaping, and reward. It represents the natural cycle of the year, especially the turning over of a new cycle. The longest nights are about to come to an end, harkening the time to reap the reward of prior hardships.

It is a representation of change, a positive change at that. If Jera shows up in a reading, understand that reward is on its way. You have toiled, suffered, undergone hardships, and braved harsh weather. Now, you may retire, take a sabbatical, or even go on a vacation.

Jera is the rune of material gain. Gebo is the rune of spiritual gain. If both runes show up in a reading, it's a sign that you're going to get both happiness in relationships and monetarily. While there will be time to work hard again, and surely you will, right now, Jera's appearance suggests that you slow down and celebrate all that you have accomplished.

ᛇ

Eihwaz

Phonetic Value: Y

Pronunciation: "AY-wahz"

Eihwaz means the Yew Tree. Moreover, it represents life and death, enlightenment, balance, renewal, and, most importantly, the World Tree.

The Yew Tree stands in a snowy field. Brave in the face of all the lifelessness around it. Ever it remains so supple and strong; ever it stays green. Its red berries supply nourishment to those who are struggling to survive in that harsh environment. Its grace and majesty are a sign of its refusal to succumb to the opposition all around it. Yew trees have had a very significant role in the occult, and even in Christianity, they represented immortality which was why they were planted in churchyards. The wood from this tree made the best bows and could kill enemies from a long range.

When Eihwaz shows up in a reading, it's telling you that change is in the air. This will be a necessary and major change that will forever change things for you. Going to college, getting married, retiring, getting a new job, changing your profession, having a baby—all these changes are huge changes that require you to brace for what's coming.

There may be different sorts of changes that can happen either one at a time or at once—material, physical, mental, and spiritual. Let these changes serve as the vehicle that takes you from one point in your life to another. Keep yourself steady, focused, and driven through this process. Think of the Yew Tree and how it remains steadfast. You need to embody that in your life.

Eihwaz is also sometimes a sign that there's going to be a problem in your life that you have to sort out in advance before it becomes something grave.

This rune cannot be reversed.

Perthro

Phonetic Value: P

Pronunciation: "PER-thro"

The literal meaning of Perthro is dice-cup. Now, what does the dice cup signify? Fate. Chance. Mystery. Secrets.

You cannot always know all the possibilities for a solution. Sometimes, no matter how hard you'll try, the future will remain shrouded in mystery until such a time when the dice is cast. What does a player do when playing a game of chance when a dice cup is involved? A player constantly remains vigilant of all the moves that his opponents have made and keeps an eye on the board, knowing that while the outcome of the dice is not changeable, the other variables on the board are very well controllable. Thus, be on the lookout for signs that the universe might be sending toward you. Someone close to you might be keeping secrets from you.

When Perthro appears inverted, it's a sign that someone will reveal an unwanted secret to you soon. Sometimes, it indicates that you'll be free of a burdening secret that was otherwise causing you mental and physical harm.

Algiz

Phonetic Value: Z

Pronunciation: "AL-geez" / "el-hahz"

Algiz depicts elk's antlers, a person with his arms upraised, or even Heimdall, who holds his sword in one hand and his horn in the other. The literal meaning of this rune is defense, sanctuary, and protection.

When interpreting Algiz in a reading, one must note that context is extremely important. While the rune does symbolize protection, this protection can either be proactive or reactive. It could be telling you that you're safe from a threat as you have already taken protective measures. That's why the context is important here because if protective measures are not taken, Algiz is a sign that you need to ward yourself against a present threat.

The defense that Algiz represents is also a spiritual defense. You have to draw upon your inner emotions and create a safe space mentally and spiritually to protect yourself from the overwhelming spiritual and mental dangers around you. Use this time to seek solitude and meditate to ascend your spirit into the echelons of divinity to protect yourself from the undivine.

An inverted Algiz is called Ihwar. Ihwar is a warning rune, telling you that you've been lax in your defenses and danger is nearer than you thought. It beckons you to take up arms immediately. Your defenses were down, and others saw this as an opportunity to attack you. All is not lost, though. If you'll listen to the inverted Algiz, you'll still manage to defend yourself.

Sowilo

Phonetic Value: S

Pronunciation: "So-WEE-lo"

Sowilo is the rune symbolizing the sun, therefore signifying health, vitality, wholeness, and good energy. Fertility follows this rune, along with positivity, happiness, and good fortune.

If you draw this rune in a reading, you'll get success and lots of it. It won't be a success in just one aspect of your life; you'll find permanent success that does not depend on the weather, unlike Jera. An example of permanent success is overcoming a serious illness for good or hitting it big in business. It's something that will help sustain you till the end of your days.

Sowilo can never be inverted.

Tiwaz

Phonetic Value: T

Pronunciation: "TEE-wahz"

Tiwaz references Tyr, the legendary God who lost his hand to Fenrir. His victory against Fenrir came at a great personal sacrifice. However, this sacrifice ensured that his people were protected, even though this meant that Tyr was rendered useless in his trade. As harsh as what happened to Tyr was, Tiwaz is a positive rune, hinting towards justice, leadership logic, masculinity, responsibility, loyalty, and sacrifice.

If this rune shows up in a reading and you were looking for a spiritual breakthrough, know that it is on the way. You'll finally be able to perceive things from an elevated perspective. If you were looking for material gain, know that there's going to be an uphill climb. You will have to give it all to your management, leadership, and dexterity if you intend to succeed in whatever venture you're engaged in right now.

Sometimes, success comes at a price. A painful price, at that. This rune can foretell danger—danger in the form of an injury or personal loss. Sometimes, this rune can foretell something grave about to happen to one's family, company, friends, or team.

An inverted Tiwaz suggests that progress through the application of force is not the wisest route in this situation. Find another way, a less aggressive route, something that tends to focus on the brain more than the brawn. A reversed Tiwaz may indicate that you're facing a lack of motivation. Maybe you're being cowardly towards a matter that requires bravery. Perhaps you're feeling overwhelmed in the face of the challenge that lies ahead of you. Again, slow down, reevaluate, and tackle the matter differently. Do not let your ego get in the way.

Berkana /Berkano

Phonetic Value: B

Pronunciation: "BER-kah-na" / "BER-kah-no"

Berkana is a feminine rune containing a lot of feminine power within its interpretation and meaning. Its literal meaning is that of a birch tree, a symbol of fertility in Norse paganism. Additionally, the shape of this rune is symbolic of the female form. Berkana represents the bond between a goddess and her creation and between a child and their mother. It's a powerful, nurturing, protecting, and supportive indication when this rune appears.

Just as Uruz contains within itself the male mysteries, all the feminine mysteries are contained within the Berkana rune.

When Berkana appears in a reading, it can represent pregnancy and the start of a person's new life. A business venture can be a fertile one, as boded by this rune. When Berkana shows up, it is the herald of good beginnings, whether in marital life, business, or in a spiritual direction. Berkana represents healing as well.

If it shows up inverted, it's hinting towards the person being stubborn and obstinate in the face of growth, stating that the person has to accept the rites of passage of life and has to grow, flow, and evolve if they intend to succeed.

Ehwaz

Phonetic Value: E

ᛖ

Pronunciation: "EH-wahz"

Ehwaz means horse and represents movement, progress, teamwork, trust, loyalty, and travel.

It motions toward forward movement and expending energy into traveling. If it shows up in a reading, it's a telling sign that you need to put in steady effort into attaining a goal. You may need to travel to attain this goal as well. Perhaps your business venture will take on a long-distance form, and you'll either have to communicate over long distances or travel to oversee the business.

If you're in a joint venture, focus on teamwork, communication, trust, and consistency to drive your venture home.

A reversed Ehwaz is suggestive of blocked movement and an inability to act. Your solution for such inaction is to evaluate the situation and gauge whether action or passivity is needed. An inverted Ehwaz also connotes failure to communicate in time. Lastly, this reversed rune represents a lack of trust on your part. Surprisingly, the rune here states that you were right all along to withhold trust from a certain person.

ᛗ

Mannaz

Phonetic Value: M

Pronunciation: "MAN-naz"

Mannaz means man or humankind at large. This is the rune of individuality, cooperation between people, kindling friendship, humanity, and helping others.

This rune is relationship-oriented, reminding us that bonding is at the heart of humanity and that we are all connected through the nature of our being human.

When Mannaz appears in a reading, it's referring to strengthening your relationship with others and thinking of your community as a whole. You will be assisted by others in a task that you need help with and will find that there's a lot of camaraderie and brotherhood in the people around you should you ask for their help.

A reversed Mannaz warns you that you have isolated yourself too much from others and have become disconnected from people, resulting in all the negativities that are going on in your life. Your feelings of depression, sadness, low energy, and dejectedness are arising from the fact that you've disconnected yourself from people. You have to reconnect with the right people, but not before healing yourself and taking the time to reorient yourself.

Laguz

Phonetic Value: L

Pronunciation: "LAH-gooz"

Laguz means water, specifically, lakes, the ocean, and seas. It represents the endless possibilities and nourishment that come with water. A ship riding the waves of the sea may end up on a new continent, leading its passengers to discover virgin lands, lands rife with possibility. It's a rune of femininity, intuition, cleansing, and unconsciousness.

This rune reminds us that it's important to have a deep understanding of ourselves. Be like water. Go with the flow. Let yourself loose. Follow your instincts. Become in tune with your feelings. That's what Laguz represents. The universe is trying to get in touch with you, revealing things that were hidden before.

A reversed Laguz indicates obstinateness, a lack of movement, and flowlessness. Are you inadvertently stopping your personal growth? Well, it's time to meditate and cultivate that growth rather than hinder it. Pursue the creative endeavors that truly fulfill you rather than indulge in those activities that are blocking your creative outlets.

Ingwaz / Ingaz

Phonetic Value: Ng

Pronunciation: "ING-wahz" / "eeng-wahz"

Meaning "seed," Ingwaz is a rune regarding reward, growth, awareness, success, and creation. More importantly, it is a rune about the earth, agriculture, and nature. It is one of the alternate names for Freyr, the god of fertility and agriculture.

This rune represents the earth and our relationship with it. It appears when someone is supposed to spend more time with nature. When Ingwaz shows up in a reading, it's telling you to pay attention to outdoor activities like gardening, sports, hiking, and swimming. Why? Because they're good for your body and mind. They're going to improve your health and, in doing so, grant you a sound mind. This personal growth is often overlooked by those who are so busy in their daily lives. Ingwaz wants you to reconnect with nature.

This rune cannot be reversed.

Dagaz

Phonetic Value: D

Pronunciation: "DAH-gahz"

Dagaz represents dawn. It is the rune of transformation, signaling the arrival of the day after a long night. It is a positive rune, signifying clarity, the triumph of good over evil, and light.

When you face challenges in your life, Dagaz's appearance states that you will overcome them with optimism and a positive outlook. This rune is a reminder of the cyclical nature of everything—night and day, life and death, rise and fall. There is an awakening hidden within the meaning of this rune. You are going to come across new possibilities and discover new worlds if you decide to align your mentality positively. This rune truly embodies the adage, "it's darkest before dawn." If you've been stuck in a rut, feeling hopeless, seeing no end to your troubles, Dagaz comes as a welcoming sign that all your troubles are going to come to an end, leaving you with new possibilities and unexpected adventures.

One cannot reverse this rune, either.

Othala

Phonetic Value: O

Pronunciation: "OH-tha-la"

This rune means property, particularly one's home, land, or estate.

This is the rune of the ancient clan lands. Historically, houses and estates have a strong spiritual link with their owner. A person is as much part of their house as the bricks and walls that make it. You build this place to live in, then populate it with memories and actions, giving it new life, every room a separate organ, and you, at the center of it all, running from room to room, living, thriving, alive, and making the house come alive with your spirit. That's why places become haunted, to begin with. The owner might not be there, but within those walls, memory is stored.

Othala is a manifestation of generational accumulation. A father builds a house that the son lives in, and so forth. In that manner, this rune is about nobility, heritage, family, history, honor, hard work, and pride. It's a rune depicting spiritual power, especially ancestral spiritual power that lingers long after the ancestor has departed from this realm.

If you draw this rune, it's telling you that you have to reconnect with your family and get in touch with your roots. You need their emotional support just as much as they need yours. When this rune turns up, you should expect wealth, prosperity, property, and land positively. Additionally, it might be a sign that you have to go back and visit the home of your ancestors and get in touch with the country of one's forebears.

Similarly, a reversed Othala suggests that there's a clash or a rift in the family that has to be immediately resolved cautiously and positively. It can be a sign that you're unable to accept family as a source of happiness in your life. In the worst case, it can be a sign that you're going to lose wealth and land.

How To Cast Runes and Read Them

Rune casting is an excellent way to hone your intuition and access your inner self, the self that is in touch with divinity. This secret self holds the key to divination. You can start by experimenting with different layout styles. Traditionally, runes were cast in multiples of 3 or odd numbers. 5 rune layouts are used commonly as well, along with some 7 and 9-rune layouts too. There's one that has 24 runes which is done at the start of each year to forecast what the year holds. Like Tarot, runes have many layout options you can experiment with, using the ones that suit you best.

At the most basic level, you can use a 1 rune pull for a simple yes and no sort of answer. The 3 runes casting is very similar to the traditional Tarot spreads, with each rune standing for past, present, future, or situation, action, and outcome.

Runes were originally cast by looking at the sky and throwing the runes on a special piece of cloth, then reading the upright landed runes.

The second most common way to read runes is to hold the rune pouch in your non-dominant hand and then think about the question that you want to be answered. Pull the runes out with your dominant hand and place them in your desired layout shape.

You can try out the following layout ideas, after which you'll be adept enough to try your own layouts:

The 3-Rune Layout

An ideal spread for beginners, the three-rune spread allows you to do a basic reading by removing three random runes from the pouch and putting them in front of you. The first rune should be on the right, the second in the middle, and the third on the left. The first one represents your overall circumstance. The second rune represents the challenges you may face, and the third one represents the action you must take in the face of the challenges.

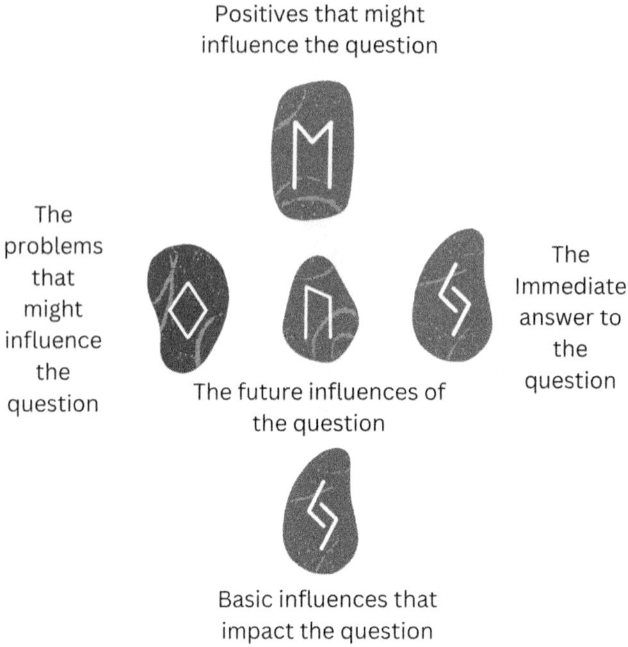

The 5-Rune Layout

Lay these runes in a cross. The rune at the bottom represents the basic influences that impact the question, while the rune on the far left indicates the problems that might influence the question. The top rune shows the positives that may influence the question, while the rune on the far right shows the immediate answer to the question. The only remaining rune is the one in the middle, which shows the future influences of the question.

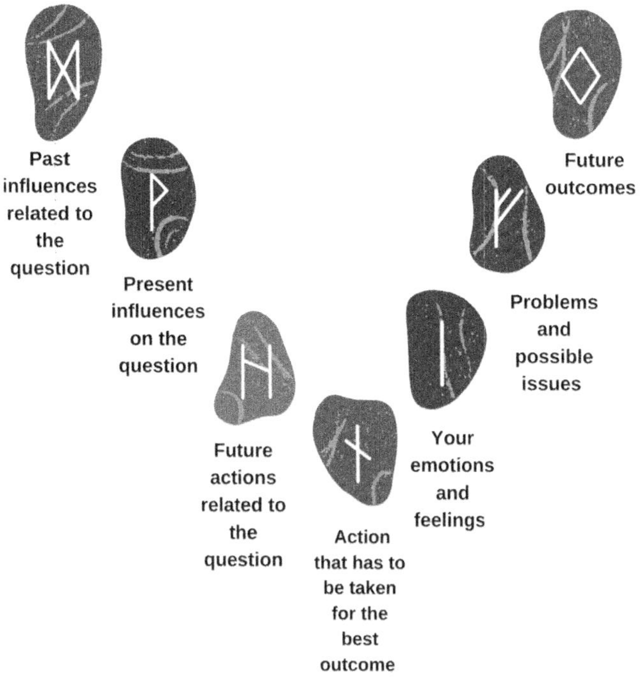

The 7-Rune Layout

This layout is laid in a V shape. The top left rune states past influences related to the question. The rune at the second from the top left shows the present influences on the question. The third rune from the top left states the future actions related to the question. The rune at the center bottom shows the action that has to be taken for the best outcome related to the question. The rune to the right of the center bottom shows your emotions and feelings related to the question. The rune second from the top right shows problems and possible issues related to the question. The top right rune shows future outcomes related to the question.

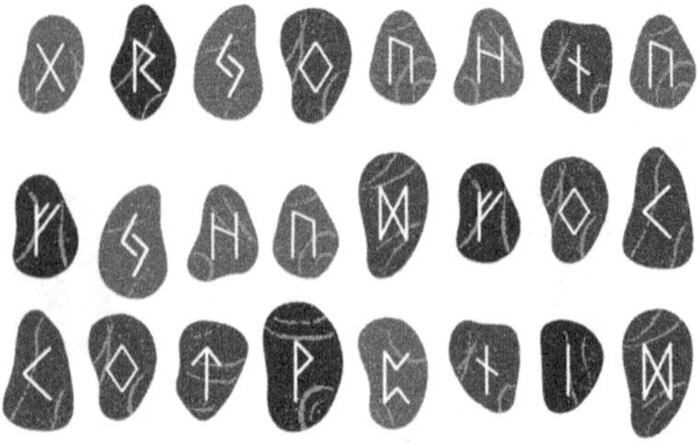

The 24-Rune Layout

Often done at the start of the year, the 24-rune layout contains exhaustive answers about, well, everything. This is done in a 3x8 grid.

The first row starting from the right to left shows:

- **First:** How you will achieve money and prosperity this year.
- **Second:** How you will achieve physical health this year.
- **Third:** How you will achieve defense or destruction this year.
- **Fourth:** How you will achieve wisdom and inspiration this year.
- **Fifth:** Which direction your life will take?
- **Sixth:** Any future wisdom that you'll learn.
- **Seventh:** The skills and gifts that you will be granted this year.

- **Eighth:** How you will achieve peace and happiness this year.

The second row from right to left shows:

- **First:** The future changes to your life.
- **Second:** The things that you need to achieve your goals.
- **Third:** The obstacles that are hindering you.
- **Fourth:** The successes and achievements that await you.
- **Fifth:** The challenges you will face and the choices you will have to make.
- **Sixth:** The inner skills that will manifest within you.
- **Seventh:** Your critical life situations this year.
- **Eighth:** Your guiding energy.

The third row from right to left shows:

- **First:** Your legal and business affairs.
- **Second:** How you will attain growth.
- **Third:** Friendships and relationships this year.
- **Fourth:** Your social status.
- **Fifth:** Your emotional status.
- **Sixth:** Sexual or romantic situations.
- **Seventh:** How you will attain balance.
- **Eighth:** Gain of assets this year.

Bind runes and How To Make Them

Bind Runes are two or more runes bound together to serve a magical purpose, such as making an amulet or to cast a spell. Combining different runes can invoke the gods for an outcome. Now, whether this outcome is good or bad depends on what runes you have used.

Bind runes bind spiritual energy into material objects for enhancement (such as a spell that can enhance someone's natural abilities) or enchantment (in the form of an amulet). Some common examples of bind runes include talismans that protect you from harm, enchanting items like weapons to become more powerful, and even empowering yourself to overcome challenges.

The two main types of bind runes are linear and radial.

Linear has two more sub-types, **stacked** (in which two runes share the same axis and are stacked upon each other) and the **same-stave** runes (in which runes are aligned along an axis). The linear ones can be used in spells to manifest a reality, while the same-stave ones can be used to attack a problem.

The r**adial bind** runes contain a combination of runes that stem from a common center point. These are used as defense spells or amulets.

You are going to mix together runes, which can result in compounded effects, unknown effects, and even completely mystical effects that are so quintessential to the mysterious nature of the runes therefore before you can make bind runes, you must first understand the meaning of each individual rune as well as their positive and negative effects.

Do not be afraid. This is ancient wisdom that you are studying and using. Your mind and spirit will be elevated as a result of using this craft. So, rather than become paralyzed with fear at the prospect of wielding this magical power, be in awe and approach this discipline with reverence. You can use the Elder Futhark that we discussed in this chapter.

Step 1. Manifest what you want to achieve.

Think about the goal of your spell. What are you trying to achieve? Is it motivation? Are you looking for strength? Do you need clarity in your journey? Are you asking the gods for help? Are you lacking in strength? First, make it clear in your head what you want to achieve. It is only after you've manifested what you want to achieve that you can begin to select the runes that you need to use. Remember, without intent and visualization, it's going to be impossible to pick up the right runes. If you pick up the wrong runes, it can lead to unwanted consequences.

A spell should have a concise goal, its intent clear, and its meaning apparent.

Step 2. Select the runes.

After you've read about all the runes, their meanings, and their effects, select the ones that suit your purpose best. Do not overcomplicate things, especially if this is your first time working with bind runes. Just choose two or three runes. At the very most, pick up five.

This is the most important part of the process, as many runes have ambiguous meanings that can clash with the effect of other runes. You do not want to make the runes work against each other. You want to make them come together and work for you. So, be patient and take your time. Study more than one resource, cross-reference the meaning of the runes and their effects from different sources, and only after you're completely satisfied with their meaning and effect, move on to the next step.

Step 3. Create the design.

First, sketch the design on paper. Create many different combinations. Don't worry about right or wrong right now. Just work with your intuition and let your imagination fly. Draw to your heart's desire and draw whatever comes into your mind.

Give the drawings some time after you're finished. Go for a walk, read a book, watch a movie, or just disengage from the process of designing. After some time, the bind rune will come to you out of the blue. Then rush back to the paper and draw the design that came to you.

If that does not happen, then go back to your drawings and pick the one that vibes with you the most. Study that one and see if there are any reversed runes in there or if any hidden runes snuck into your drawing. These can alter the meaning of the spell. Re-draw the design without the unwanted runes and then finalize it.

• • •

Step 4. Select the material.

If you want the bind runes to serve a long-term purpose, choose wood, stone, or metal. Ideally, something that can stand the test of time. If you just want to do something for the short-term, even cardboard can suffice.

If you want to create a pendant or amulet, choose comfortable jewelry you can wear for a long time without discomfort.

Step 5. Creating the bind runes.

It's time to give power to your bind runes. Before carving the bind runes, consecrate a space by lighting a candle and incense. Meditate in this place and clear your mind and align your intentions.

Then, carve the runes individually, thinking about how each rune's meaning and effect can help you, and then join these together in the final design.

Once you are done, meditate again and think about the intent of this bind rune, whether it's an amulet or a carving. In the end, thank the gods and goddesses you have invoked for their help. Leave an offering for them.

Step 6. Using the bind runes.

Use the bind runes carefully. If you have an altar at home, place the bind runes there and make sure they are nearby and at hand. Keep your bind rune close until you achieve the goal that you set out to attain. Once that has happened, you can get rid of the bind rune. If it's paper, burn it. If it's wood or stone, bury it or cast it into a lake. Just make sure you don't cause any pollution.

Thank the gods and goddesses once more after you've achieved your goal and leave another offering for them. How you can leave offerings for the gods and goddesses and how you can venerate them will be discussed in great detail in the upcoming chapter.

Storing the Runes

If you have runes in your possession, know that they must be treated with care and respect. If you do that, you'll find that the runes are very powerful allies. They have to be cleaned and empowered and stored properly.

It's critical to clean them, especially if they are new and have been touched by many hands before. They are considered a personal item. You need to keep them with you as much as possible so that they can tune into your personal energy, allowing them to give you more accurate readings.

When cleaning them, you should wait for a full moon night and then place them outside for the entire night. You can also leave them in the sun for twenty-four hours if you want. You may smudge them with wafting smoking herbs like sage and lavender and releasing their purifying properties to clean the runes. Lastly, you can clean them with natural water from a river, creek, stream, spring, or well. Never use tap water for that purpose.

After they're cleaned, you must empower them. Empowering can be done by laying out the runes in the midday Sun and then retrieving them at dusk. You can also place the runes on a piece of cloth and then sprinkle sea salt on them to empower them with the element of Earth. Then, run the runes through incense smoke while empowering them with Air. You should then pass them through a candle flame to empower them with Fire. Lastly, sprinkle rainwater or spring water on them to empower them with Water. Empowering has to be done regularly if you work with the runes frequently.

Store them in a bag made of natural fiber like cotton or silk. Use an exclusive bag for them, as the bag comes into contact with the runes and contains their pure energy. That bag is their home. You may use a piece of fabric for wrapping the runes and for laying down as the casting cloth.

This chapter was extremely thorough and quite lengthy, but given the subject matter, this was required. Now, you have a detailed insight into what the runes are, how they originated, what they mean, how to cast them, how to bind them, and how to store them.

Not only did we study each rune in detail, we learned about different casting methods. Your takeaway from this chapter should be to practice the casting and binding as much as possible while re-examining the meanings and effects of the runes. The more you are in tune with the runes, the better you'll be able to cast and the better you'll be able to bind them.

Treat this discipline with the reverence and respect it deserves, as runes are extremely powerful in terms of magic, spirituality, and mystical potency. This is just the beginning of our foray into the world of Norse Magic. In the next chapters, we will examine different rituals such as Seiðr, Spá, and Galdr. We'll discuss how we can incorporate Norse magic into our daily lives, how to build altars, and how to practice rituals like Blót and Sumbel.

CHAPTER 7
NORSE MAGIC

Unlike the profaned status that magic has been relegated to today because of Christianization and the dominance of Abrahamic faiths, wherein magic has been cursed as the art belonging to the devil and demons, in the Old Norse world, magic was revered as a part of nature, an elemental force that could help people see into the future, shift into other forms, and fathom the mysteries of the universe. It was as much a part of the Norse folks' life as hunting, raiding, and farming was. While there were practices within magic that were seen as off-limits (perceived to belong to the gods and goddesses and not to men and women), magic was at large a regular part of the community, with people inviting the practitioners into their homes or visiting them for all sorts of things, whether they were related to divining the future or asking the favor of the gods for better crops, or even victory over their enemies in the battlefield.

The Norse folk respected the practitioners of magical arts greatly, often coming to them for their services. Predominantly, magic was seen as a feminine craft, although men did partake in it as well. But in doing so, they recognized that they were adopting a feminine craft. For the men, adopting magic sometimes meant endangering their masculinity in the eyes of the community. There are exceptions to this rule, of course, even in mythology. Odin learned how to perform seiðr from Freya, who was the best in the business. But that had more to do with Odin's quest to become more knowledgeable than anyone else.

The reason why magic was seen as a woman's art in those days was that women were seen as holy vessels imbued with magical powers and possessing the capability of reaching out to the divine for prophetic purposes. This reverence for womenfolk endured in Scandinavia until Christianity arrived, which was and remains to this day, a thoroughly patriarchal religion.

Before Christianization, magic was considered a part of the everyday life of the Norse folk. It wasn't seen as blasphemous or unholy. Quite the opposite, actually. Those who were able to divine the future were thought to possess the ability to communicate with the gods and the Norns. The Norse practitioners of magic used their understanding of the world and their perception of the gods to decipher dormant truths laid out in the world and in the cosmos. For them, magic was a force like any other force, and it could be used to discern destiny, foresee the future, and shape someone's fate.

A völva or gyðja—a divine seeress—would carry out magical rites, rituals, blóts, and other ceremonies. The magicians were also known as seiðkonur or spákonu, which meant the ones who "speak" and "send." The men who delved into magic were known as goðar, galdramaðr, or seidhmadhr.

Seiðr

The translation of this Nordic word means to seethe or to send. Magical practices that were related to divination, astral projection (also known as soul travel), channeling the soul sheath, necromancy, and even cursing someone. There was a ceremonial and esoteric nature to seiðr, with much of it being somewhat similar to shamanic rituals.

A völva could perform more than just the art of divination. Besides seeing into the future, she could put curses, lift them, form protective boundaries that saved someone from physical and spiritual harm, and even manipulate destiny in some cases. The völva could cast benign spells as well, such as love spells, spells for prosperity, and charms that had to do with friendship and loyalty.

When seiðr was performed in a group setting, the rites were called utiseta (which involved sitting out) and the völva's song (in which vocals were utilized to raise collective energy). The spoken incantations were called galdr, which were used to reach altered states of consciousness. These states would also be ecstatic in nature and could be used to get in touch with the spirits of one's ancestors, as well as other spirits. In these altered states, the völva would ask questions while divining, and the spirits would help her perceive the answer.

One particularly powerful aspect of seiðr was to change fate, the principle being that if you could see the future, you could take steps to avoid that future from coming into being, therefore changing the course of destiny, and the second principle being that the use of magic changed the course of fate by making events happen that otherwise would not have happened, eventually changing fate.

The archaeologist Neil Prince provided a good summary of seiðr. He said that the seiðr rituals were concerned with clairvoyance and seeking out hidden truths within the mind and in physical locations. According to him, seiðr could be used to heal the sick, bring good luck, control the weather, for calling animals and fish for hunting, and divination. But these were benign uses of seiðr, as per his summary. He said that seiðr could be used with malevolent intent by cursing someone, blighting the land and making it barren, inducing illness, killing someone, telling false futures, injuring people, and invoking hate in someone's heart for another.

Mythologically, seiðr was seen as the domain of the Norns, who used magic of many kinds to tell the shape of the future of all living beings. But among the gods and goddesses, Freya and Odin were seen as the foremost authorities on seiðr.

Historically, the völva used to wander from town to town and farm to farm. There, they would come across people who'd commission them to perform acts of magic in exchange for room, money, board, animals, or anything else that the völva would ask for. The most popular story concerning a völva comes from the saga of Erik the Red.

In his saga, a völva was asked to come to a steading so that she could divine for the people when their famine would end. Upon her arrival, she was treated with much respect and given a meal comprising the hearts of animals that were difficult to hunt.

Then, she sat in a raised seat that had a cushion made from hen feathers. A woman sang a song to invoke the spirits who'd help the völva go into a trance. The völva prophesied when the famine would end and answered other questions for other members of the steading. She was adorned with a specially crafted costume and wielded a staff with a brass knob.

This tale shows us that the völva was set apart from the rest of society, both exalted and reviled at the same time. It also provides us with a basic framework for how seiðr works. A seeress sits on an elevated platform to perform her magic. Chants are sung to bring the seeress into a state of trance and the subsequent prophesizing.

When it comes to performing seiðr, there are three main steps to follow.

- The **first step** involves learning about the altered states and gradually going into them, i.e., going into trance. Sometimes, the act of going into a trance is also known as seething (which is one way this practice got its name) because, in this state, the person convulses a lot. In the first step, you have to learn how to block out the world around you and focus on just the ritual itself. Go inwards, meditate, and seek within yourself. This is not meant to be vague advice. This is exactly what you have to do. Following the fundamental principles of meditation, you must first empty your mind, regulate your breathing, and then let yourself be empty of all thoughts. In the old days, sometimes the völva would use herbs and drugs to get into a trance-like state. The mystical nature of the song sung to them by their assistant would also catalyze their going into a trance. The song served to open the doors to the otherworld and to let the seeress become more immersed in her meditation.

- The **second step** is concerned with soul-traveling. This is done after the trancelike state is attained. Most of the work the seeress performs is done in this state. This stage is also called faring forth, path walking, journeying, and sitting out, as in sitting outside of your body, walking the spiritual path, faring forth into the realm of wights, and journeying into the mystical dimension of souls. It is a complex but intuitive part of the process wherein you will have to direct yourself where you have to go. If you're going to answer questions about the future, you'll have to fixate on the person who is answering the questions. In case you're performing it for yourself, you'll have to direct your focus within yourself. In this stage, spirit guides and animal totems can come to your aid to assist you with your questioning. They're also called the fylgja, animal forms that accompany you throughout your life. With enough practice, a seeress or a shaman performing siedr can even shape-shift (first in an astral capacity, then later, potentially in physical form as well). You can even perform spirit possession in this state, where you can allow your body to be a vessel for the gods, goddesses, and spirits, who can then work through you.

- The **last step** is about rhythm. A rhythm throughout the ritual can help you maintain the trance as well as come out of it. The singer, often the assistant to the seeress, would sing rhythmically, first creating a rising tempo in her song and later subside it to reach a trough that would prompt the seeress to come out of her altered state. A drum would also be used, its initial striking forceful and fast, and its ebb slow and deliberate. The rhythm is used to further one's concentration when performing seiðr. It controls the ritual's pace and dictates when it starts and ends.

Spácraft

Yet another form of spiritually focused magical practice, spácraft, was considered more practical and much more readily accepted by the people. This form of magic was practiced by women who were deemed to have healing abilities and a psychic inclination.

Spácraft /Spá could determine orlog through intuition or meditation. The spá-kona were the practitioners of this magic form and could use it to foretell the future and one's fate by directly interacting with the strands of the wyrd.

Historical records, such as the one written by Tacitus, tell of a prophetess named Veleda, who prophesied the victory of the Vikings over the Romans. She said that there would be an uprising that would result in success for her tribe. In the end, what she had prophesied came to pass, thus granting credibility to this practice in a historical context.

Another example of spácraft was when Thorgeirr, the Lawspeaker, went under the cloak for two days and then gave a prophecy about Iceland's religious future in which he saw the Christianization rapidly spreading through the area. To preserve the religion, he suggested that the Norse lore be written down and preserved. Had it not been written down, much of what we know today would have been lost.

Practicing spácraft is relatively simpler than performing seiðr or galdr. It is even easier if one has a psychic inclination. Spácraft was seen as a matter of psychic sensing without the utilization of much skill or effort. If you want to practice it, start by paying attention to your sixth sense and to any feelings of foreboding that come your way. Say you get an intuitive thought about an event coming to pass. Write it down. A few days, weeks, or months later, if that event does come to pass, know that you have an innate ability for spácraft. Now, to become adept at it, there is more to it than paying attention to your personal emotions and observing outside omens. You need to be able to do it at will.

To perform spá at will, you have to tune in to your intuitive and psychic abilities and focus them on a particular question or problem. You may fixate your thoughts on the matter and gather all the emotions that you feel when you think about that particular event. If those emotions remain uniform for a while, note them down. Do this for several different questions, events, and forebodings. Notice how your accuracy goes up almost tangentially the more you practice spá. When you start practicing spá, begin with smaller events. The upcoming results of an exam, for instance. Start from the microscopic before you learn to foresee the macroscopic.

Because of its similarity to seiðr, spá, and seiðr had a lot of overlap in both a historical context and in the present context. The two schools of thought in this matter state that a) either spá is a specialized form of seiðr meant to be practiced by only those who have earned the title of völva or b) that spá is a more positive aspect of the same soul work of which seiðr is a darker aspect, that they're two sides of the same coin.

Given that spá was used to prophesize the results of battles, harvests, sailing, childbirth, trading, and foretelling an individual's fate, one can see how the two forms are similar.

Spá wasn't always all about intuition. Sometimes, trancework techniques were also performed, such as mound sitting (in which the practitioner sat upon a burial mound) to communicate with the dead.

Galdr

Galdr involved singing incantations. The songs sung during this practice were considered to be imbued with magical powers. Surprisingly, this bit of magic was not exclusive to the Norse people. Performing magic through singing—especially singing in varied notes—was common practice in Indians, Indigenous Americans, Arabs (particularly pre-Islamic Arabs), and in the Aztec civilization as well.

A common misconception regarding galdr is that they were used to vocalize the sounds and meanings of the runes. While that was one form of galdr, it was hardly all that galdr constituted. Those who performed galdr used more than just runes. Songs could be sung to venerate the deities, elements of nature, one's ancestors, and other spirits.

While men who practiced seiðr and spá were considered to be ergi (unmanly), they weren't considered so when they practiced galdr, as it was considered a craft fit for both genders. In some instances, it was considered to be a more masculine form of Norse magic, with men being preferred to perform it as opposed to women.

Most of the formal incantations were performed in the poetic meter of galdralag, the meter of spells. But there were also cases where impromptu and extemporaneous songs were sung to perform galdr. It was all about poetic composition and how one could creatively use words to wield the power of poetic language in the form of song.

In many cases, women sung to delivering mothers to ease their childbirth. In other cases, someone could be rendered mad by singing a particularly chaotic song to them. Gven the musical portfolio of some modern pop singers, it's understandable how someone could be driven mad by a mere song.

A master of galdr could, through their singing, make sharp swords blunt, make distant ships sink, raise storms, bring about drought, and even decide the victory or defeat of an army.

Many Eddas mention galdr by name. Odin is said to know 18 galdrar in Hávamál.

The principle of galdr extends beyond just singing or chanting. It is more than just stringing together notes and hoping for something to happen. There is pattern, rhythm, intent, and form. When these are combined for a single purpose, the song manifests a tangible magical change.

Domestic and Healing Magic

In Norse culture, spinning is connected to fate and magic. Even the web of fate is said to have comprised many threads woven together. Spinning had religious philosophy behind it. People believed that the goddesses of spinning inspected the distaffs and spindles of women of a household and judged her as either industrious or lazy, rewarding the former with good luck and punishing the latter with disaster. The skill of a spinning woman automatically dictated the luck of the family.

This belief extended very exhaustively toward the children. The people believed that the fate of a child could be made, changed, and even harmed through spinning. The Swedish women would draw blood from their fingers in the seventh month of their pregnancy. They would use a sewing needle and then use the blood to mark a strip of wood with protection spells and symbols. Then they would spin linen thread that was dyed red, black, and white. This strip was burned, and its ashes were mixed with beer or mead. A burning twig was taken from the fire and used to burn apart the linen threads. Later on, the three threads would be used for individual purposes. The white cord was used to tie off the umbilical cord of the baby. The red one was tied around the baby's wrist for protection. The black one was burned to ashes, and then the ashes were buried. The afterbirth was buried under the tree on which the linen threads were dried.

Spindle whorls were discovered by archaeologists that acted as prisms when spun in the sunlight.

Magic could be woven into clothes as well for protection.

Beyond household magic, pagan societies applied it in healing as well, for the treatment of physical and mental illnesses. This was done in the form of amulets and curing stones. Curing stones were used to ease childbirth and staunch bleeding, as well as granting wishes to the wearer and making them invisible.

A mother would lay her hands on her son before a battle and would divine where he'd get wounded in the battle. The son would then take extra caution to protect those particular body parts, thus saving himself from a terrible fate.

Although these were the main forms of magic used by the Norse people, this list is far from exhaustive. Sadly, many such magical traditions have been lost with time. Today, we have an inkling of an idea about the kind of magic that the Norse folk used, but we do not possess the full picture.

Luckily, modern revivals such as Ásatrú and Vanatru have not only revived the old practices of magic but also added their own flair to the practices to keep the tradition alive while also innovating just about enough to keep the practices compatible with the times.

It is my belief that all that is lost is not lost forever. The gods and goddesses once communicated with the people thousands of years ago and directed them in their lives, taught them magic, and provided them with sustenance. I believe that they still do it today if one's intent is pure and one's connection is sincere.

In the next chapter, I'll discuss how to venerate the gods to open a line of communication with them.

Who knows, maybe the once-lost rites and rituals will make it back to us by communicating with the gods directly.

CHAPTER 8
PRACTICING NORSE MAGIC

This chapter deals with practical magic, which includes a step-by-step guide to working with the gods, performing blót and Sumbel, and understanding how naming ceremonies and weddings were also rituals that were imbued with magic at their core.

Working with the gods

In the Hávamál, the 144th stanza summarizes the skills needed for runecraft while also laying down the groundwork for Norse religious practices.

Do you know how to carve, do you know how to interpret,

Do you know how to stain, do you know how to test out,

Do you know how to ask, do you know how to sacrifice,

Do you know how to dispatch, do you know how to slaughter?

The first two verses, as stated by the High One, indicate towards carving, interpreting, staining, and testing out the runes. The next two encapsulate the essence of Germanic religious practices.

Do you know how to ask? This refers to supplication. One can ask the gods for anything. A good harvest, healthy progeny, success in endeavors such as battles, and so forth.

Do you know how to sacrifice? The word in the original text is blóta, which refers to sacrifice. Back in the olden days, this referred to the sacrifice that had to do with bloodletting and dedicating meat to the gods and eating it.

Do you know how to dispatch? A more fitting word for the translation would be to send. As in, do you know how to send? This indicated to the sending of something to the gods. The next line clears it up as to what is being sent.

Slaughter. People slaughtered anything from animals to their foes in battle to send to the gods.

The two main elements that come into light from these verses are prayer and offerings.

Praying to the Gods

Prayer, according to the Old Norse religion, was the act of communicating with the gods rather than merely worshipping them. The words and acts involved in performing a prayer varied significantly.

One prominent example of a prayer was the greeting the Valkyrie Brunhild used for Sigurd.

Hail to thee Day, hail, ye Day's sons:

hail Night and daughter of Night,

with blithe eyes look on both of us,

and grant to those sitting here victory!

Hail Æsir, hail Asynjur!

Hail Earth that givest to all!

Goodly spells and speech bespeak we from you,

and healing hands in this life!

Here, the prayer includes requests and salutations. We can get a blueprint of what a prayer constitutes from this passage. It hails the powers that identify the god, attracts their attention by declaring their traits, and honors them through veneration. Brunhild requests skills in communication and in performing magic. She does this by calling upon the powers of nature and the gods and goddesses as a whole.

There's also a prayer to Thor preserved in Snorri Sturluson's work by skalds, who prayed to him by saying:

You smashed the limbs of Leikn;
you bashed ðrivaldi;
you knocked down Starkadhr;
you trod Gjalp dead under foot.

Historian John Lindow compared this prayer to other surviving prayers from Indo-European traditions, stating that such prayers included two components of praise to the god, followed by a request to that deity.

From this, we can construct a formula for prayer, which can be something like this:

Hail (to the god using their best-known name), (a descriptive epithet),

Child of (their parent's name), lover of (their spouse's name)

You who dwell in (the name of their hall),

You who (summarize their deeds),

With your (their weapon or tool)

Come quickly to aid me,

As I (state your problem)

Invoking a god's help can be done through chanting their names, referencing their attributes and their monickers, and even stating out loud their endeavors from their mythologies.

Offering to the Gods

Praying to the gods was just one part of paganism. One of the oldest practices of their faith was to offer things by way of sacrificing to them. Besides blood sacrifice, food was offered to the gods as well as any offerings that the worshipper deemed suitable and fitting for the god. For example, grain, flowers, fruit, alcohol, and hair cut from the forelock were some of the primary offerings. You could even offer a verbal vow as an offering.

When animals were sacrificed, their heads, hearts, and hides were also hung as offerings while their blood was poured on the shrine and sprinkled on the people. The meat from those animals was consumed in a communal feast.

These sacrificial feasts were also part of the yearly traditions and festivals that marked the turning of a season, weddings, funerals of noblemen, or even to gain the favor of the gods in times of disaster.

When sacrificing animals, special care was taken to ensure that the animals were healthy and perfect in every way. The animal was washed and garlanded with aromatic herbs and flowers.

Today, heathens offer a diverse range of offerings as a sacrifice, which include:

- Nuts
- Fruits
- Meat
- Cheese
- Butter
- Mead
- Beer
- Spirits
- Animal Effigies
- Baked goods
- Grains

It's important to note which god and goddess prefers which gift.

When making an offering to Freya, effigies of animals like cats, boars, falcons, rabbits, and horses would do wonderfully. She'd also love naturally shed cat hair or claws. You can offer her mead, wine, and honey. Perfumes are another of her favorite offerings. A goddess of sensuality, she has a special corner in her heart for aphrodisiacs like chocolate and strawberries. She's also got quite the sweet tooth and loves apples and raspberries. Additionally, you can offer her silver, gold, copper, necklaces, and stones like emerald, jade, citrine, and amber. As I said earlier, you can also pledge a vow as an offering. When it comes to Freya, if you vow to care for cats or to devote time of your day to taking care of local flora, she'll be very pleased and inclined towards you.

The gods and goddesses have a certain affinity for discipline. Dedicating an altar space for them and placing altar offerings for them is yet another surefire way of getting them to notice you.

When you devote an altar to Odin, you'll be, in a sense, offering him a gateway to come to you. You can set up the altar by decorating it with the Hanged Man tarot card, the Othala rune, the Ansuz rune, raven feathers, effigies of wolves, horseshoes, mead bottles, and beer. The All-Father is also fond of red meat, tobacco, and spirits.

You must understand that modern Norse Paganism does not condone human sacrifice and acknowledges that those practices were inhuman practices that have no place in modern paganism today. People are not a resource to be given away.

. . .

Performing Blót

Considered the most sacred and most important ritual in Paganism, performing a blót requires some pre-planning and understanding of what it means. The literal translation for blót is sacrifice.

But why should we blót?

Offering something to the gods isn't necessarily a transactional dynamic. You can consider blót as a device to engage in the gifting cycle with the gods. And what is a gift? When you gift someone something, you do not expect something in return. There is no obligation there. Showing the gods that you acknowledge them, love them, and venerate them through gifting offerings to them is one of the primary reasons why we do blót.

It's not like the gods need our gifts or sacrifices. They have existed long before us, and they'll exist long after us. So it's not like they're dependent on our offerings. We give to the gods because they give to us. By offering things to them, we're reflecting their divinity to them, letting them know that we're also capable of generosity and goodness.

Even though there's no obligation, the gods have your back. They're good for it. They will come to your aid with their generosity and their benignity; of course, they will. They will give you something back tenfold or even a hundredfold. That's their nature. They like to reward those whom they deem good, honorable, and sincere. They like to gift back.

Sacred Space

Performing a blót requires access to a sacred space, and since most of us do not live in the vicinity of temples, you can designate a certain area as a sacred space by performing ritual purification. It is in this space that you and your fellow pagans can feel safe, guided, protected, and comfortable conducting the blót.

For this purpose, you can use a natural spot in the woods, a room in a community center, your backyard, or any space where you can connect with your fellow venerators and with the gods.

Performing the Blót

For the blót, we're going to need the following things:

- Mead as an offering (beer can work too)
- A drinking horn
- A bowl for collecting the libation
- Sprig of evergreen

The worshippers have to stand in a circle facing each other inwards.

Start by pouring the beverage into the horn and invoking the god/goddess that you wish to invoke. Raise the horn and say the toast to the deity. Then drink from the horn. Pass the horn around to everyone in the circle, and one by one, they have to raise and toast and drink.

After the horn has reached the first person, pour some of it as a libation in the bowl.

Now do another round of drinking, this time toasting the heroes of yore. Pour the remaining libation into the bowl.

Do a third round for boasts and toasts, then pour the remaining as a libation in the bowl.

Dip the sprig in the mead bowl and sprinkle the people with the mead, using the sprig as a blessing.

Lastly, pour the libation onto a sacred spot.

A Modern Variant

You can add a modern twist to the blót, such as the one Ásatrú members have been practicing since the 2000s.

In this variant, you need an offering (see the list mentioned earlier), a beverage that can be offered as a libation, a bowl to catch the libation, and a sprig of evergreen for aspersion.

You also need fire and water for blessing and for purifying the sacred space as well as the offering.

You can use candles or torches for the fire. Additionally, if the sacred space has room for it, a brazier or fire pit can be used for the sacrificial fire.

For the water, a single jug of clean water can be used so that everyone can wash their hands and face before touching the offerings.

You can stand around the sacrificial fire in a circle, or you can all stand on one side of the fire while the goði stands near the fire. Both formations are completely fine.

For the modern version of the blót, first, set up the sacrificial fire with some wood. You can use an accelerant for this purpose as well. Now pour some fresh water into a jug and also get a bowl for the water.

Whatever offerings you have planned to sacrifice, gather them together. Then, distribute torches or candles to the people gathered for the offering. Light these candles and walk over to where the sacrificial fire is going to be. You can now hand the torch to the goði so they may light the sacrificial fire.

Pour some water into the bowl and let the goði wash their hands and face. Dispose of that water.

Let the goði speak a prayer that may invoke the gods and goddesses. Following the prayer, the supplicants should pray, chant, sing, and dance as the goði sanctifies the offerings at the sacrificial fire.

Now, these offerings may either be placed at the fire, or they can be left out on an altar. If libation is involved, it should be poured out and caught in the bowl for the blessing.

It is at this time that the dancing should stop. Around this time, when the offering is being made, you should kneel or prostrate as you see fit. While the sacrifice is happening, the chants and the songs should continue until it is done.

The goði will leave the sacred space, bless the gathered people, and announce the beginning of the feast.

Sumbel

The Sumbel, also spelled as symbel and sumbl, is the practice of sitting together and drinking together. Participants pass the horn to each other as they make toasts and boasts and vow oaths. They also make speeches, give gifts, form alliances, make agreements, and hear each other's oaths.

The Sumbel was used to strengthen pre-existing bonds and form new ones within a holy setting. While a blót can be done alone, Sumbel is entirely communal.

The religious significance of this ritual was to boast your past deeds, your ancestor's past deeds, and the deeds of the great heroes so that those who have passed might live on through their memory. Oaths and promises made during the Sumbel took on a more sincere and strengthened form, allowing the individuals and the group to shape their wyrd. To ensure sincerity, Sumbel made sure that those who made false promises or words without worth were punished through a distorted shaping of their wyrds that would eventually bring them harm.

The intent behind the Sumbel is to celebrate the community, strengthen it by bringing it closer together, and venerate one's gods and ancestors by boasting about them. It is by venerating them in such a communal spirit that one's ancestors can take place within the Sumbel like visitors, and the gods can be harkened to witness this ritual.

Performing Sumbel

The ritual demands that you sit, unlike standing, which is done in blót. Sumbel also takes place indoors, unlike blots, which can be performed both indoors and outdoors. In the sagas, it was described that halls had rows of benches and high seats. The head of the hall sat at the high seat while others sat on the benches. Today, however, Sumbel is performed by sitting in a ring, rectangle, or any other shape wherein you can sit facing others while remaining close enough to them.

Since it's exclusively a drinking-related ritual, Sumbel was historically arranged after dinner. It usually begins by offering a basin of water and a towel to the gathered people so they may wash and dry their hands.

Whether it's ale, cider, beer, wine, or mead, the Sumbel begins with the filling of the drinking vessel with the preferred drink. Then the leader speaks a blessing or a prayer (in some cases, both) over the filled horn and then toasts. This toast is traditionally made to a god or goddess or a group of them, such as the Æsir and the Vanir. This toast can be something as simple as Hail Thor! Or it can be something as complex as a full-fledged poem written in skaldic meter. The leader then swallows the drink, in response to which the assembled people also say hail!

Then the horn is passed from one person to the other. If it's a larger gathering, the horn goes around the room via a horn-bearer who gives each person the horn, hears their toast, acknowledges it, and then takes the horn to the next person. In the end, the horn-bearer gives their toast.

After the first round, the drink leftover from the drinking vessel is poured into the blessing bowl to give the gods their due.

There can be three rounds of drinking, one for the gods and goddesses, the other for the heroes and ancestors, and the third for anything that the participants choose.

. . .

Naming Ceremony

A name is considered a gift that gives the newborn its status as a human being and a member of the family. Historically, the father took the child, sprinkled water on the child, and named them. This was called ausa vatni, which means sprinkling of water.

The materials required for a naming ceremony include a pitcher of water, a cloak for the parent to wrap the child, the naming gift, and a ceremonial bowl, preferably one that belongs to the family. For the procession, you'll need the godparents, the father's parents, the mother's parents, and the parents with their newborn child. In Asatru the goði, performs the salutations and invocations. After the salutations are said to the guests, invocations are made to Freya, the Alfar, and the Disir, and then the water is poured into a bowl by the officiants.

The godparents present the child with the name-fastening gift and place it next to the water bowl.

The grandmothers approach the baby and recite the blessings of the Disir:

Hail the dead.
Hail the wives, mothers and sisters.
Hail our ever-faithful friends!
Look on us
with kind eyes,
That we may
Bless a new life and name.

The child is given a first and middle name.

The grandfathers then approach the baby and recite the blessing of the Alfar:

Hail the dead.
Hail the husbands, fathers and sons.
Hail our ever-faithful friends!
Look on us
with kind eyes,
That we may
Bless a new life and name.

The child is then given a family name.

The priest comes forth holding the naming gift over the child, then recites the blessing Freya:

Hail, day!
Hail, sons of day!
Hail night and her daughter!
Look on us
with kind eyes,
That we may
Bless a new life and name.
Hail Aesir,
Hail Asynjor,
Hail the holy giving Earth,
Bless us with goodly speech and wisdom
And healing hands in life.
Hail Freya Vanadis.
Hail Gracious Lady.
Hail Queen of the Disir.
Look on us
with kind eyes,

That we may
Bless a new life and name.
Hail the Joyful One.
Hail Frith Weaver.
Hail Luck Bearer.
Bless us with goodly speech and wisdom
And healing hands in life.

The priest then gives the newborn to the father, who'll fold the child in his cloak. The mother is given the water bowl.

The parents then recite the blessing of the sprinkling of water. They name the child with the full name and sprinkle the newborn's head with water.

Wedding Ceremony

Let's break down the wedding ceremony into ten steps. Note that this is a modern paganistic reconstruction of the original Norse wedding rites.

- Receiving the guests
- The Hallowing of the Rite
- Attesting to the characters of the bride and groom
- Invocation of the gods
- Speaking the Oaths
- Giving Gifts
- The Blessing of Thor
- Announcing the Couple
- Commencing the Feast
- The Honeymoon

Receiving the guests

It begins by receiving the guests at the entrance of the venue and inviting them in. Following the guests, the couple comes in.

Back in the old days, the woman passed from her father's protection to her husband's. Today, you can see this reflected in the modern custom where the father walks the bride down the aisle and gives her away.

Hallowing a rite

The leader of the ceremony begins this ceremony by announcing the purpose of the ceremony.

Witnessing the characters

The family members of the couple are asked to speak about the man and woman's good qualities and their suitability for marriage to each other.

Invocation of the gods

Now, this is where the magic comes in. First, the leader invokes the gods and goddesses, and then the ancestors of the couples so that they may come and hear the oaths and bless the marriage.

Speaking the oaths

The woman brings a horn of drink to the man, who drinks it, then takes her hand and swears his oath. The woman can do this as well. The remaining drinks from the horns are then placed into a bowl as an offering to the gods.

Giving gifts

Both partners give each other gifts. Historically, weapons were exchanged, wedding bands given, and keys to the house given by the groom to the bride to signify that she now held dominion over the household. In modern times, you may choose suitable gifts of your choosing.

The blessing of Thor

Thor's hammer should be placed on the bride's lap to hallow the ceremony. The hammer is also a phallic symbol meant to signify fertility in the upcoming days. This invokes Thor, who turns his attention to the wedding and blesses it, being the patron god of the Midgardians.

Announcing the couple

The leader then pronounces the man and woman as married.

Commencing the feast

The men and the women from both sides of the family race to the feasting hall. Those who lose have to serve the drinks to the winners. Once at the feasting hall, mead is drunk, and food is eaten, while much talk is had and songs are sung.

Honeymoon!

The couple is then sent forth on their honeymoon, preferably with some honeyed mead so that they can drink, loosen up, and get in the marital mood, so to speak.

You might wonder why I included the naming ceremony and the wedding ceremony in a chapter related to magic rituals.

Well, what is magic, if not the utterance of special words, invoking the deities, and performing a ritual to bring about a certain manifestable change in the world? Is the naming of a child, not a change? When the destinies of two people intertwine to become one, isn't that a change brought about by invocation, supplication, and performing the necessary rites?

The Norse understood that magic was imbued in their everyday lives, from the most ordinary thing, such as tilling soil, to the most special rite, such as marriage.

In this chapter, we learned how to work with the gods through offerings and prayers. We discussed how to perform blót in detail and then did the same for Sumbel. Lastly, we looked at two major rites, the naming ceremony and the wedding ceremony, and understood them within the context of the rituals that they are in that they involve supplication, offerings, veneration, and praying.

You might be wondering where to go from here, given that there is such a rich reservoir of information that you can access and implement in your life, from divining runes to performing rites strengthened with magic.

On that note, intuition was considered a magical trait in Norse Mythology. It still is. Intuition is one form of wisdom, an innate wisdom that can serve to guide you when the paths are many and the directions are vague.

The hardest part is to begin. Once you do begin, let your intuition guide you. Use this book as a reference and find your way to the gods and goddesses. Divine the mysteries of the secret world all around you, the world where Jörmungandr still stirs around the world, where Sleipnir strides across the skies, and where Thor prompts lightning to fall by wielding his hammer.

That world is not lost. It's still there. Just as your ancestors are still there, living inside you. Just as the gods and goddesses are still there, watching over you. Just as you are here, uncovering this ancient truth, the greatest of truths—that the magic is real! It was always real all along.

THANK YOU

Thank you for letting me be your guide through the fascinating history and mythology of the Norse. Now, I'm sure you're wondering how you can help others experience the same joy and fulfillment that you have gained from reading this book.

Leaving a review can be a great way to help others learn about Norse Paganism. Your review can help people discover the book, and it provides an opportunity to share your own experience and what you've learned on your journey. All you need to do is >>Click here to leave a quick review

If you are reading this in hardback or paperback, type in this link on your device: https://amzn.to/4b72cgX or scan the QR code below!

AFTERWORD

If you think that this is the end of our journey together, it is not. We may yet meet again, whether as fellow travelers on this great road that we call life or as readers and writer again in a different narrative.

When I set out to write this book, I had one goal in mind. I wanted to make sure that you, the reader, would discover as much as you could about the wonderful world of Norse Mythology, understand the pantheon of the Norse gods and goddesses, and learn how to harness your knowledge of mythology and paganism in its many forms and utilize it in your daily life.

I would be all too glad to learn from your feedback if I have managed to achieve my goal.

Let us review what we have learned so far in this book.

- We began with an introduction to Norse Magic, wherein we discussed, among many things, Odin and his tale of sacrifice, what magic is, what power language possesses, and how mystery and history are intertwined when it comes to Norse Paganism. I briefly shared some details about me as well as discussed why you should read this book.

- Then we went back to the beginning of it all, to the beginning of Norse cosmology. We understood the distinction between folklore, myths, and legends. Then we dived into the history of the world, from the Ginnungagap to the creation of the Nine Realms.
- No mention of Norse Paganism, Magic, and Mythology would be complete without shedding light on the Nine Realms and the World Tree. In the second chapter, we looked at each realm in detail.
- In the third chapter, we looked at the gods who helped shape these worlds and then resided in them. From the Æsir, such as Odin and Frigg, to the Vanir, such as Nerthus and Kvasir, we took a look at the major gods of the Norse pantheon before taking a deep dive into the A-listers of Norse Mythology.
- In the fourth chapter, we studied Odin, Frigg, Thor, Baldur, Vidar, Tyr, Bragi, Idun, Loki, Heimdall, Njord, Freya, Freyr, and Mimir. This encompassed their histories, their traits, and their powers.
- We got to the meat of the book in chapters five and six. The fifth chapter was all about Norse Paganism and what it entailed. We discussed its characteristics, the beliefs that it espoused, and the rituals that were performed by the pagans.

- In the sixth chapter, we dwelled upon runes, first going through their history, then looking at each and every symbol, meaning, and usage. We learned how to cast runes, bind runes, and store them.
- In chapter seven, I introduced you to various elements of Norse Magic, such as seiðr, spá, and galdr, while shedding light on domestic and healing magic.
- In the final chapter, we discussed how some rites were practiced back in the day and how we can practice them today. These included working with the gods through prayer and offerings, blót, Sumbel, the naming ceremony, and the wedding ceremony.

I will admit that a book of this length cannot be exhaustive when it comes to teaching magic, helping you divine the runes, while also teaching you everything about Norse Mythology and Paganism. But I have tried, and in my humble attempt, I have sought to give you a framework that you can use to adapt more magical practices in your daily life, perfect the ones that you've already learned about through practice, and understand the principle and the reasoning behind the many rites and rituals of Norse Paganism.

The accounts told within these pages are not just stories. They are legends and myths from an era that has long since passed but whose ethics, values, and beliefs still live on in the hearts and practices of thousands of modern-day pagans. With the information provided in this book, you too can become a practicing Norse pagan and strengthen your connection with the Norse gods and goddesses. They are seeking you just as you are seeking them.

The purpose of providing such extensive historical accounts and facts was to prepare you for the future. Now that you know about the history of runes, their symbology, and their meaning, you can use them for runework, such as divination and binding magic.

With the historical context of seiðr, blót, Sumbel, spá, and galdr clear to you, you are more than capable in my eyes of carrying out those rites and rituals to transcend and communicate with the gods.

If you'd like other readers and kindred spirits such as yourself to find this book better, please do consider leaving a helpful review. This review will also help me and will allow me to write further books exploring Norse mythology, paganism, rituals, and rites in more detail.

Thank you for embarking on this journey with me. And remember, this is not goodbye. We may yet meet again.

But until then, farväl!

RESOURCES

THE NORDIC BIG BANG

- Where do myths, legends and folktales come from? (2019, March 15). Retrieved March 13, 2023, from https://www.torch.ox.ac.uk/article/where-do-myths-legends-and-folktales-come-from
- How did our legends really begin? (2014, July 29). Retrieved March 13, 2023, from https://www.independent.co.uk/arts-entertainment/books/features/how-did-our-legends-really-begin-9634148.html
- How the great myths and legends were created. (n.d.). Retrieved March 13, 2023, from https://writersstore.com/blogs/news/how-the-great-myths-and-legends-were-created
- Mark, J. (2023, March 13). Mythology. Retrieved March 13, 2023, from https://www.worldhistory.org/mythology/
- Myths and legends of the world. (2023, March 13). Retrieved March 13, 2023, from https://www.encyclopedia.com/humanities/news-wires-white-papers-and-books/norse-mythology
- Groeneveld, E. (2023, March 10). Norse mythology. Retrieved March 13, 2023, from https://www.worldhistory.org/Norse_Mythology/
- Norman. (2018, June 30). The origins of the Norse mythology. Retrieved March 13, 2023, from https://thenorsegods.com/the-origins-of-the-norse-mythology/

- Skjalden. (2022, July 18). Creation of the world in Norse mythology. Retrieved March 13, 2023, from https://skjalden.com/creation-of-the-world-in-norse-mythology/
- The history of the Nordic region. (n.d.). Retrieved March 13, 2023, from https://www.norden.org/en/information/history-nordic-region
- The creation of the cosmos. (2018, July 24). Retrieved March 13, 2023, from https://norse-mythology.org/tales/norse-creation-myth/

THE NINE REALMS

- Mark, J. (2023, March 10). Nine realms of norse cosmology. Retrieved March 13, 2023, from https://www.worldhistory.org/article/1305/nine-realms-of-norse-cosmology/
- Milligan, M. (2021, August 26). Yggdrasil and the 9 norse worlds. Retrieved March 13, 2023, from https://www.heritagedaily.com/2018/08/yggdrasil-and-the-9-norse-worlds/121244
- Ásgard and the nine worlds of Norse mythology. (n.d.). Retrieved March 13, 2023, from https://www.history.co.uk/articles/asgard-and-the-nine-worlds-of-norse-mythology
- Muspelheim. (n.d.). Retrieved March 13, 2023, from https://www.britannica.com/topic/Muspelheim
- Niflheim. (n.d.). Retrieved March 13, 2023, from https://www.britannica.com/topic/Niflheim
- Midgard. (2018, June 30). Retrieved March 13, 2023, from https://norse-mythology.org/cosmology/the-nine-worlds/midgard/
- Vanaheim. (2017, July 09). Retrieved March 13, 2023, from https://norse-mythology.org/cosmology/the-nine-worlds/vanaheim/

- Jötunnheim. (n.d.). Retrieved March 13, 2023, from https://kids.britannica.com/students/article/Jötunnheim/311926
- Svartalfheim. (n.d.). Retrieved March 13, 2023, from https://godofwar.fandom.com/wiki/Svartalfheim
- Hel (the Underworld). (2017, July 09). Retrieved March 13, 2023, from https://norse-mythology.org/cosmology/the-nine-worlds/helheim/
- Alfheim. (2017, July 09). Retrieved March 13, 2023, from https://norse-mythology.org/cosmology/the-nine-worlds/alfheim/

Chapter 3 —The Pantheon of Norse Mythology

- HistoryExtra. (2022, August 30). A brief history of the Vikings. Retrieved March 13, 2023, from https://www.historyextra.com/period/viking/vikings-history-facts/
- Delgado, D. (2020, May 29). Legendary characters from Norse mythology. Retrieved March 13, 2023, from https://www.megainteresting.com/history/gallery/legendary-characters-from-norse-mythology-741590756208/1
- Vanir. (n.d.). Retrieved March 13, 2023, from https://www.newworldencyclopedia.org/entry/vanir
- Aesir. (n.d.). Retrieved March 13, 2023, from https://www.newworldencyclopedia.org/entry/aesir
- The aesir-vanir war. (2018, July 04). Retrieved March 13, 2023, from https://norse-mythology.org/tales/the-aesir-vanir-war/
- Owen.pham. (2022, July 01). The difference between the Aesir and Vanir. Retrieved March 13, 2023, from https://www.wondriumdaily.com/the-difference-between-the-aesir-and-vanir/

THE A-LIST GODS OF NORSE MYTHOLOGY

- Smith, M. (2022, February 22). 15 Norse mythology gods and goddesses list - with names & info. Retrieved March 13, 2023, from https://education.onehowto.com/article/norse-mythology-gods-and-goddesses-list-13342.html
- A guide to norse gods and goddesses. (1970, October 29). Retrieved March 13, 2023, from https://www.centreofexcellence.com/norse-gods-goddesses
- Seven of the most important gods and goddesses in Norse mythology. (n.d.). Retrieved March 13, 2023, from https://www.history.co.uk/articles/seven-of-the-most-important-gods-and-goddesses-in-norse-mythology
- The norse gods. (n.d.). Retrieved March 13, 2023, from https://thenorsegods.com/
- Gods and creatures. (2018, July 14). Retrieved March 13, 2023, from https://norse-mythology.org/gods-and-creatures/
- The aesir gods and goddesses. (2018, September 04). Retrieved March 13, 2023, from https://norse-mythology.org/gods-and-creatures/the-aesir-gods-and-goddesses/
- The vanir gods and goddesses. (2018, September 04). Retrieved March 13, 2023, from http://norse-mythology.org/gods-and-creatures/the-vanir-gods-and-goddesses/

NORSE PAGANISM

- Routes North. (2022, June 20). Norse paganism: What is it, and what do its followers believe? Retrieved March 13, 2023, from https://www.routesnorth.com/language-and-culture/norse-paganism/
- The Old Nordic Religion Today. (n.d.). Retrieved March 13, 2023, from https://en.natmus.dk/historical-knowledge/

denmark/prehistoric-period-until-1050-ad/the-viking-age/religion-magic-death-and-rituals/the-old-nordic-religion-today/

- Nomads, T. (2023, January 05). Norse paganism for beginners: Quick introduction + resources. Retrieved March 13, 2023, from https://www.timenomads.com/norse-paganism-for-beginners/
- Pagan religious practices of the Viking Age. (n.d.). Retrieved March 13, 2023, from https://www.hurstwic.org/history/articles/mythology/religion/text/practices.htm
- Staff, Sigurþórsdóttir, S., Gunnarsson, O., & Helgason, M. (n.d.). 11 things to know about the present day practice of ásatrú, the ancient religion of the Vikings. Retrieved March 13, 2023, from https://icelandmag.is/article/11-things-know-about-present-day-practice-Ásatrú-ancient-religion-vikings
- Mythology. (n.d.). Retrieved March 13, 2023, from https://www.cliffsnotes.com/literature/m/mythology/summary-and-analysis-norse-mythology/the-norse-gods-8212-odin-thor-balder-frey-freya-and-loki
- Lafayllve, P. (2022, August 31). Modern Norse pagan practices for beginners. Retrieved March 13, 2023, from https://www.spiritualityhealth.com/norse-paganism-for-beginners
- Nikel, D., Warren, R., Evelake, Paula, Heimdallr, Raven, . . . Brown, D. (2020, December 03). Viking religion: From the Norse gods to Christianity. Retrieved March 13, 2023, from https://www.lifeinnorway.net/viking-religion/?__cf_chl_rt_tk=Ns7il0FW1D9MkUis2eT7mt2WF55N.Cq1iX_nROH3eR8-1678716442-0-gaNycGzNCtA

THE RUNES

- Rune guide - an introduction to using the runes. (n.d.). Retrieved March 13, 2023, from https://www.holisticshop.co.uk/articles/guide-runes
- Groeneveld, E. (2023, March 10). Runes. Retrieved March 13, 2023, from https://www.worldhistory.org/runes/
- Shelley, A. (2023, March 01). Futhark runes: Symbols, meanings and how to use them. Retrieved March 13, 2023, from https://andreashelley.com/blog/futhark-runes-symbols-and-meanings/
- Talisa + Sam | Two Wander. (2022, September 27). Rune meanings and how to use rune stones for divination. Retrieved March 13, 2023, from https://www.twowander.com/blog/rune-meanings-how-to-use-runestones-for-divination
- Wigington, P. (2020, January 31). What is rune casting? origins and techniques. Retrieved March 13, 2023, from https://www.learnreligions.com/rune-casting-4783609
- Nomads, T. (2023, January 29). Rune magic 101: What are and how to make bind runes. Retrieved March 13, 2023, from https://www.timenomads.com/rune-magic-101-what-are-and-how-to-make-norse-bind-runes/

NORSE MAGIC

- Women and magic in the sagas: Seiðr and spá. (n.d.). Retrieved March 13, 2023, from http://www.vikinganswerlady.com/seidhr.shtml
- Owen.pham. (2022, September 03). Magic in old norse: Seith, curses, and blessings. Retrieved March 13, 2023, from https://www.wondriumdaily.com/magic-in-old-norse-seith-curses-and-blessings/

- Manea, I. (2023, March 11). Viking witches and Norse Magic. Retrieved March 13, 2023, from https://www.worldhistory.org/video/2735/viking-witches-and-norse-magic/
- HistoryExtra. (2023, February 01). Gods, myths and rituals: What we know about viking religious beliefs. Retrieved March 13, 2023, from https://www.historyextra.com/period/viking/viking-religion-gods-myths-rituals-ship-burial-sacrifice-odin-thor-loki/
- Seidr. (2018, July 04). Retrieved March 13, 2023, from https://norse-mythology.org/concepts/seidr/
- Garis, M. (2021, March 15). How to make a home altar that honors your personal power. Retrieved March 13, 2023, from https://www.wellandgood.com/how-to-make-altar-home-design/
- Basics of Sumbel. (n.d.). Retrieved March 13, 2023, from http://www.thewhitegoddess.co.uk/articles/general_pagan/basics_of_sumbel.asp

PRACTICING NORSE MAGIC

- Worshipping the gods. (2012, April 09). Retrieved March 13, 2023, from https://hrafnar.org/articles/dpaxson/norse/worship/
- Blot: Heathen rituals. (n.d.). Retrieved March 13, 2023, from https://thetroth.org/resources/rituals/blot-Ásatrú-rituals.html
- Symbel: Heathen rituals. (n.d.). Retrieved March 13, 2023, from https://thetroth.org/index.php/resources/rituals/symbel
- Naming ceremony: Ausa Vatni. (n.d.). Retrieved March 13, 2023, from https://thetroth.org/resources/rituals/naming-ceremony

- Ásatrú wedding ceremony. (n.d.). Retrieved March 13, 2023, from https://thetroth.org/index.php/resources/rituals/Ásatrú-wedding-ceremony

Printed in Great Britain
by Amazon

43560571R00118